THE WAY
PEOPLE
LIVE

Life in the Elizabethan Theater

Titles in The Way People Live series include:

Cowboys in the Old West
Life During the French Revolution
Life in Ancient Greece
Life in Ancient Rome
Life in an Eskimo Village
Life in the Elizabethan Theater
Life in the North During the Civil War
Life in the South During the Civil War
Life in the Warsaw Ghetto
Life in War-Torn Bosnia
Life on a Medieval Pilgrimage
Life on an Israeli Kibbutz

THE WAY PEOPLE LIVE

Life in the Elizabethan Theater

by Diane Yancey

Lucent Books, P.O. Box 289011, San Diego, CA 92198-9011

Library of Congress Cataloging-in-Publication Data

Yancey, Diane
    Life in the Elizabethan Theater / by Diane Yancey.
        p.   cm. — (The way people live)
    Includes bibliographical references and index.
        Summary: Discusses theater in sixteenth-century England, describing
    playwrights, plays, the audience, and Queen Elizabeth's sponsorship.
        ISBN 1-56006-343-2 (alk. paper)
        1. Theater—England—London—History—16th century—Juvenile
    literature.   2. Theater—England—London—History—17th century—
    Juvenile literature.   3. Theater audiences—England—London—History—
    16th century—Juvenile literature.   4. Theater audiences—England—
    London—History—17th century—Juvenile literature.   5. English drama—
    Early modern and Elizabethan, 1500–1600—History and criticism—
    Juvenile literature.   6. English drama—17th century—History and
    criticism—Juvenile literature.   [1. Theater—England—History.
    2. English drama—History and criticism.]   I. Title   II. Series.
    PN2596.L6Y36   1997
    792'.09'031—dc20

                                                    96–33400
                                                    CIP
                                                    AC

Contents

Discovering the Humanity in Us All

The Way People Live series focuses on pockets of human culture. Some of these are current cultures, like the Eskimos of the Arctic; others no longer exist, such as the Jewish ghetto in Warsaw during World War II. What many of these cultural pockets share, however, is the fact that they have been viewed before, but not completely understood.

To really understand any culture, it is necessary to strip the mind of the common notions we hold about groups of people. These stereotypes are the archenemies of learning. It does not even matter whether the stereotypes are positive or negative; they are confining and tight. Removing them is a challenge that's not easily met, as anyone who has ever tried it will admit. Ideas that do not fit into the templates we create are unwelcome visitors—ones we would prefer remain quietly in a corner or forgotten room.

The cowboy of the Old West is a good example of such confining roles. The cowboy was courageous, yet soft-spoken. His time (it is always a he, in our template) was spent alternatively saving a rancher's daughter from certain death on a runaway stagecoach, or shooting it out with rustlers. At times, of course, he was likely to get a little crazy in town after a trail drive, but for the most part, he was the epitome of inner strength. It is disconcerting to find out that the cowboy is human, even a bit childish. Can it really be true that cowboys would line up to help the cook on the trail drive grind coffee, just hoping he would give them a little stick of pep-

permint candy that came with the coffee shipment? The idea of tough cowboys vying with one another to help "Coosie" (as they called their cooks) for a bit of candy seems silly and out of place.

So is the vision of Eskimos playing video games and watching MTV, living in prefab housing in the Arctic. It just does not fit with what "Eskimo" means. We are far more comfortable with snow igloos and whale blubber, harpoons and kayaks.

Although the cultures dealt with in Lucent's The Way People Live series are often historically and socially well known, the emphasis is on the personal aspects of life. Groups of people, while unquestionably affected by their politics and their governmental structures, are more than those institutions. How do people in a particular time and place educate their children? What do they eat? And how do they build their houses? What kinds of work do they do? What kinds of games do they enjoy? The answers to these questions bring these cultures to life. People's lives are revealed in the particulars and only by knowing the particulars can we understand these cultures' will to survive and their moments of weakness and greatness.

This is not to say that understanding politics does not help to understand a culture. There is no question that the Warsaw ghetto, for example, was a culture that was brought about by the politics and social ideas of Adolf Hitler and the Third Reich. But the Jews who were crowded together in the ghetto cannot be understood by the Reich's politics. Their life was a day-to-day battle for existence, and the creativity and methods they used to prolong their lives is a vital story of human perseverance that would be denied by focusing only on the institutions of Hitler's Germany. Knowing that children as young as five or six outwitted Nazi guards on a daily basis, that Jewish policemen helped the Germans control the ghetto, that children attended secret schools in the ghetto and even earned diplomas—these are the things that reveal the fabric of life, that can inspire, intrigue, and amaze.

Books in the The Way People Live series allow both the casual reader and the student to see humans as victims, heroes, and onlookers. And although humans act in ways that can fill us with feelings of sorrow and revulsion, it is important to remember that "hero," "predator," and "victim" are dangerous terms. Heaping undue pity or praise on people reduces them to objects, and strips them of their humanity.

Seeing the Jews of Warsaw only as victims is to deny their humanity. Seeing them only as they appear in surviving photos, staring at the camera with infinite sadness, is limiting, both to them and to those who want to understand them. To an object of pity, the only appropriate response becomes "Those poor creatures!" and that reduces both the quality of their struggle and the depth of their despair. No one is served by such two-dimensional views of people and their cultures.

With this in mind, the The Way People Live series strives to flesh out the traditional, two-dimensional views of people in various cultures and historical circumstances. Using a wide variety of primary quotations—the words not only of the politicians and government leaders, but of the real people whose lives are being examined—each book in the series attempts to show an honest and complete picture of a culture removed from our own by time or space.

By examining cultures in this way, the reader will notice not only the glaring differences from his or her own culture, but also will be struck by the similarities. For indeed, people share common needs—warmth, good company, stability, and affirmation from others. Ultimately, seeing how people really live, or have lived can only enrich our understanding of ourselves.

"A Great National Utterance"

In cobblestone inn-yards and roughly built playhouses, an extraordinary development took place in England in the 1500s. At that place and time, genius and opportunity unexpectedly combined to produce a burst of literary achievement never before or again witnessed in the history of drama and the theater.

The Renaissance, the cultural revolution that began in Italy in the 1300s, helped spark that movement, inspiring scientific and artistic creativity throughout England. Influenced by Renaissance models and an enlightened ruler who gave the movement a royal stamp of approval, a group of men began writing dramas that portrayed life more realistically and imaginatively than ever before. Those men eventually created a notable body of work that captured the attention of the world and changed the character of drama for all time.

The Red-Haired Queen

The queen, a Renaissance woman, was the motivating force that spurred the growing excellence of the Elizabethan theater. Elizabeth Tudor, the red-haired younger daughter of Henry VIII, had been crowned queen of England on January 15, 1558, when she was just twenty-five years old. During her forty-

A Golden Age

The Elizabethan era was a time of energy and innovation, of larger-than-life adventurers such as Francis Drake and Walter Raleigh, and of villains such as the earl of Essex, who led an unsuccessful attempt to overthrow Elizabeth in 1601. Lacey Baldwin Smith describes how that energy affected the arts, particularly the theater, in The Horizon Book of the Elizabethan World.

"Nowhere was the exuberance and passionate intensity of sixteenth-century English life expressed more eloquently than in the Elizabethan theatre, where a motley company of part-time scholars, occasional actors, scapegrace brawlers, and inspired hacks reinvented a language and used it to create a literature of incomparable richness, variety, and power. . . .

Such men as Marlowe, Jonson, [and] Shakespeare . . . transformed a medieval theatre of stilted morality and mystery plays into a vehicle of expression such as the world had not seen. . . . The great period of English drama is often called the age of Shakespeare, but it would have been a golden age even if Shakespeare had never existed."

Shakespeare recites Macbeth *before an avid Queen Elizabeth. Theater reached unparalleled heights during Elizabeth's reign.*

five-year rule, known as the Elizabethan age, England flourished. As one historian writes, "If the success of a monarch can be measured in terms of rewarding victory, prosperity of the people, deepening respect abroad, and intense popularity at home, no reign can be more fortunate than Elizabeth's."[1]

Elizabeth not only provided the economic security that allowed her subjects the time and means to appreciate the arts, she supported the theater directly as well. An avid playgoer, she demonstrated to her subjects that drama was worthy of their attention and their support. At court she surrounded herself with writers, musicians, scholars, and playwrights, encouraged them in their artistic efforts, and—by her attention—promoted their prestige throughout the country and the world.

The Playwrights and Their Audience

The playwrights were the instruments by which the Elizabethan theater was lifted to unparalleled heights. Men like Shakespeare,

Christopher Marlowe, and Ben Jonson dared to write plays about real people in a variety of real situations, a welcome change from traditional English plays, which had always relied strongly on religious themes. Through their efforts, these men produced dramas that were far more sophisticated and entertaining than ever before, and audiences expressed their pleasure by demanding more and more plays.

The playgoers themselves were a significant stimulus to the remarkable flowering of the theater. The plays expressed the Elizabethans' tastes, their new love of learning, and their interest in the world. The English had long been play enthusiasts; without their continued support, the innovations of the playwrights and the greatness of the theater might have gone unnoticed and unappreciated.

"The Activities of the Age"

The Elizabethan theater did not achieve glory or fame without obstacles and opponents, however. Elizabethan audiences risked fire and plague, constant urban hazards. And while those who flocked to the theaters saw

Elizabeth I was an extraordinary woman as well as a great queen. Yet she had her idiosyncrasies, described by Lacey Baldwin Smith in The Horizon Book of the Elizabethan World.

"Only a queen could indulge an ego the size of Elizabeth's. She thrived on—and demanded—constant compliments, professions of adoration, and gifts from those around her. She encouraged her subjects' veneration [devotion], accepting the grossest and most obvious flattery with relish, and took it amiss when her ladies in waiting seemed more interested in an attractive courtier than in herself; the courtier reciprocating their attention often lost favor. The queen was inordinately vain; even when her beauty had gone and her hair had faded, her passion for sumptuous clothes and costly jewelry to 'set off' her figure and face did not abate. She wore a different dress almost every day; when she died she left some two thousand dresses and a treasure of jewels."

Although an extraordinary and popular ruler, Queen Elizabeth has been described as "inordinately vain."

the plays as outstanding entertainment, others considered them the ultimate evil. Leading the list of critics were religious leaders and city officials who felt that the theater was a bad influence on the country. "The cause of plagues is sin . . . [and] the cause of sin are plays,"[2] wrote Thomas Wilcocks, a London preacher, in 1577. "[Plays contain] nothing but unchaste matter, lascivious [immoral] devices . . . and ungodly practices,"[3] charged the lord mayor of London in 1590.

With the death of Elizabeth, the glory of the Elizabethan theater waned, and its adversaries succeeded in closing the playhouses in 1642. While the theater flourished,

however, as author and historian Felix Schelling points out, it "focused the activities of the age in itself and was literally a great national utterance."[4]

The theater reflected the preferences and preoccupations of the audiences as they came to watch the plays. It expressed the talents of the actors who trod the stage and the innovations of the playwrights who created the dramas. How these groups combined to leave a lasting mark on the theater and on the world, despite the facts that their lives were short and their outlook was centered around a single fascinating woman, is the story of life in the Elizabethan theater.

Miracles and Moralities

Life throughout England was a difficult and dangerous proposition during the Middle Ages, the historical era in western Europe that preceded Elizabeth's reign. Many people were poor tenant farmers, often living at the mercy of wealthy landowners. Houses were small, dark, and dingy. People threw filth of all kinds into the streets, and tolerated fleas, lice, and rats in their homes and clothing. Disease and death were a part of everyday life, and many children did not live through infancy. In his play *Troilus and Cressida*, William Shakespeare lists some of the ills for which there were no effective cures: "Now, the rotten diseases of the south [syphilis], the guts-griping, ruptures, . . . loads o' gravel i' the back [kidney stones], lethargies [stroke], cold palsies, raw eyes, dirt-rotten livers, wheezing lungs, . . . incurable bone-ache . . . take and take again such preposterous discoveries!"[5]

Mummery and Miracle Plays

Poverty, disease, and hardship did not stop the English from enjoying plays and other entertainments, however. Everyone enjoyed mummery—the funny actions of masked and disguised characters (predecessors of actors) who appeared at banquets and country fairs beginning in the Late Middle Ages, about 1300. Mummers never spoke; their function was to add color and gaiety to a celebration rather than to act out a story. In small villages,

mummery was often as simple as dressing a cooperative youth in a covering of leaves to represent the spirit of summer at a May Day festival. In time, mummers' performances became more complex, evolving into what can be considered simple, pantomimed plays.

Life in Elizabethan times was difficult and dangerous. Elizabethans sought a reprieve from their harsh lives by attending plays and other entertainment.

Although mummery was imaginative and enjoyable, it did not involve dialogue. Other plays that did include speaking parts—the miracle plays—were written by priests and schoolmasters at about this time. These plays were acted out by members of the local parish during a church ceremony. "The English drama, like the drama in other countries of Western Europe, began in the service of the Church, and at first was merely symbolic and a part of ceremonial [the service],"[6] notes Felix Schelling.

Most of the works were known as miracle plays because they reenacted miracles from the Bible. An example of one of the earliest is described by theater expert C. Walter Hodges. It is a simple scene, designed to be acted out on Easter Sunday.

An empty tomb is set before the altar steps. Two young priests dressed as angels stand beside it, and they are met by three others who are supposed to be the three holy women who went early to the tomb of Christ on the first Easter morning. "Whom do you seek in the sepulchre?" asks one of the angels. "We seek Jesus of Nazareth, who was crucified," reply the women. "He is not here: he is risen," say the angels, and they take the folded grave-clothes from the empty tomb and hold them up to show.[7]

Many of the earliest miracle plays were performed in Latin or given Latin titles. Latin was integral to both church and school activities, even during Elizabethan times. Priests read and spoke Latin during church services. Scholars studied Latin in the universities. Most school textbooks and other popular books on morals and philosophy were written in Latin. "Latin, Latin, and yet more Latin; it is for that the grammar school and [the schoolmaster] absolutely exists,"[8] says historian William Stearns Davis.

Mummers, with their funny masks and disguises, added color and pageantry to fairs and other celebrations.

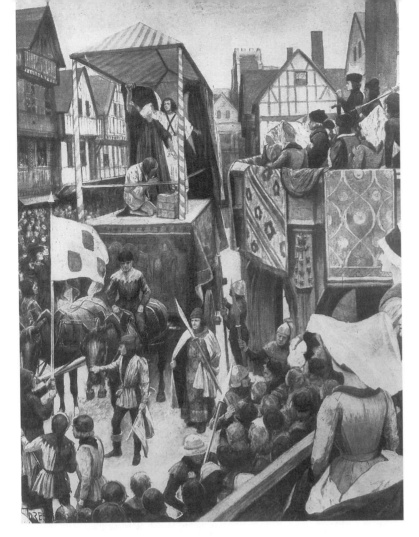

Miracle plays often portrayed miracles from the Bible and were usually performed in churches. As their popularity swelled, the plays were performed outdoors to accommodate larger audiences.

Merchant and Craft Guilds

Miracle plays were designed to be more inspirational than entertaining, but as time passed, they became so popular that churches grew overcrowded, and the plays had to be performed outdoors. Workers were recruited to build a raised stage or platform so that the people in the rear of the audience could see over the heads of those in front. With more room and larger audiences, the writers were inspired to develop more complex plays, involving more characters. People from the parish were called on to act in the various roles. Eventually entire villages took part in the performances.

In London, Norwich, and some of the larger towns, merchant and craft associations, called guilds, began writing and designing scenes for the plays in the fourteenth century. Each guild controlled and promoted a single specialized craft, so the religious scene that each put on often reflected that craft. As Hodges explains: "Thus the Bakers presented the Last Supper, and Shoemakers the long journey of the Flight into Egypt, and the Masons and Carpenters the building of the Temple."[9]

The Power of Guilds

The guild system was very powerful during the Middle Ages. There were guilds for almost every trade and craft, and their influence reached beyond on-the-job behavior. A description of some rules governing members of the bricklayers guild, taken from Marchette Chute's biography Ben Jonson of Westminster, *shows how restricting the system could be.*

"Every aspect of a bricklayer's life was thoroughly regimented. His hours of work [twelve hours in the summer and from dawn to dusk in the winter, with an hour off at noon and half an hour at three o'clock] and his behavior were covered by law, and even his bricks had to be exactly nine inches long. . . .

The system not only guaranteed each master bricklayer a supply of free labor but it also prevented younger men from setting themselves up in competition against their elders. Each apprentice had to be twenty-four years old before he could leave his master's service, a provision that was . . . designed to prevent 'over-hasty marriages and over-soon setting up of households of and by the young folk.' In return for working seven years in another man's household, the apprentice eventually reaped his reward. He became a member of the guild and could take apprentices in his turn, and, in the London area, he became a citizen of London."

The Pageants

Competing with one another, the guilds turned many miracle plays into real extravaganzas, with multiple scenes, detailed sets, and lavish costumes. Inventive townspeople soon came up with the idea of constructing large platformed wagons on which sets could be built. A wagon base was elevated above a man's head for better visibility, and the undersection was curtained off and used as a changing room for the actors. Since audiences watched from windows and street corners, sets were open on all sides. These pageants, as the wagon sets were called, were pulled by men or animals down the streets, rather like floats in a parade. At various prearranged spots they stopped while the play was performed, and then resumed their progress through the town.

In most cases, scenes were made more realistic with simple props, such as a manger for the Bethlehem story or flowers and small fountains for a scene representing heaven. At times sets became quite elaborate; enthusiastic builders were known to construct temples or even ships on the pageants. One of the most frequently used and popular sets was a monstrous head with a gaping mouth, known as a hell-mouth, designed to express the pain and terror of Satan and hell. As historian Felix Schelling explains, "The imaginative realism of the age found its vent in the yawning jaws of hell-mouth, the chains and instruments of torture and the blazing fire, and in the din and the antics of the devils and demons."[10]

Costumes for actors on these wagon-size sets were more or less elaborate depending on available money and the ingenuity of the participants. At times, characters had to make do with their own clothes. In other productions, designs were more imaginative and materials more lavish. For instance, Adam and Eve wore white leather and fig leaves in a scene depicting the Creation, while the townsman who represented the devil was dressed as a serpent.

Oddly enough, in many cases actors dressed inappropriately in costumes typical of medieval England. For instance, in a biblical scene set in the Holy Land, the apostle Paul was outfitted in a full suit of armor rather than the simple robe and sandals that were common in New Testament times. Apparently both actors and audiences accepted the notion that people of all eras and all countries wore nothing but English clothing.

The Moralities

By the fifteenth and sixteenth centuries, the church ceased to have control over most plays. The plays were no longer performed in Latin, and their themes were more secular, or worldly. Their titles reflected this change; instead of *Story of the Creation of Eve* or *Abraham and Isaac*, the audience was invited to watch *The Castle of Perseverance* and *The Disobedient Child*. The plays still concerned serious themes of good and evil, right and wrong, and thus became known as morality plays, "composed to teach the moral and religious duties of human beings."[11] No longer literal depictions of biblical episodes, morality plays taught correct behavior and beliefs by presenting allegories, or symbolic stories, about human virtues and vices. Characters in such plays, given names like Envy, Pride, and Anger, personified these qualities. Biblical characters sometimes appeared, but writers often developed these characters to make them funny or more dramatic. King Herod, for instance, became a braggart. Noah's wife became a scold. The devil, one of the most popular characters, was given parts that made him seem less and less sinister, until eventually he became a comedian rather than a villain.

Audiences were fascinated by these presentations. Although the church disapproved of their increasingly nonreligious character, it had little control over the plays now, since guilds and town councils paid for them. Not surprisingly, the cost of some of the most elaborate productions—in labor and materials for costumes, pageants, and sets—was enormous, which sometimes meant great financial sacrifice by all involved. Nevertheless, the plays were popular and generated civic pride, so productions continued. Soon townspeople were putting them on for all kinds of secular occasions, as, for instance, when nobility passed through the town, or when victorious soldiers returned from war.

Professional Entertainers

The increasing complexity and length of the plays required that players become more skilled in their performances, but actors in the miracle and morality plays were almost always amateurs. Records show that some were paid a small fee for their services; one reports a generous three shillings paid to "the performer of God," another four pence allotted to a presumably less demanding role, "hanging Judas."[12] Yet, when a play ended, most performers went back to their carpentry or their bread baking, content to leave the world of acting behind until the next festive occasion.

During the sixteenth century, however, some of these amateurs decided to make performing in plays their sole occupation. Sometimes these professional actors (they were always men) joined forces, formed acting companies, and spent their time traveling from town to town, offering their services to any and all people who wished to be entertained. They carried with them a few costumes, simple props, and a repertoire of short plays that they wrote themselves. Often staged during a break in a larger amateur performance, these short plays came to be known as interludes—something that fills time between two events—and were so popular with audiences that they became a stock part of performances of the day.

Popularity with an audience was no guarantee that the players would be accepted by town officials, however. The early actors had no established trade and no regular source of income; classed as tramps, they were often run off by town constables who suspected them of begging and thievery. As historian Felix Schelling writes: "In earlier times, the actor . . . was popularly regarded as little better than a vagabond. . . . [H]e had no fixed habitation, but strolled about the country carrying his fardle [bundle or pack]."[13]

An Outspoken Woman

The players would have waited longer for social acceptance if Elizabeth I had not come to the throne in 1558. Not every English subject liked Elizabeth, but few would have called her ordinary. The queen was intense, intellectual, and hard to please, a strong-willed and outspoken woman who ruled in an

As more and more people became fascinated by plays, traveling stages were constructed so that performances could reach more audiences. These mobile presentations eventually gave way to theaters.

The popular Queen Elizabeth surrounded by her subjects. Elizabethan theater best expresses the rich culture of English life during the reign of Elizabeth.

era when women were silent, especially when it came to public matters such as religion or politics.

Elizabeth encouraged, even goaded, adventurers such as Sir Francis Drake and Sir Walter Raleigh to explore unknown parts of the world and to lead expeditions that plundered Spanish ships. She swore at her counselors when they offered her advice that she did not like, and gave speeches that awakened great national pride in her subjects. As British author and professor A. H. Dodd notes, "The whole age [was] coloured by the rich personality of the queen herself."[14]

"My Lady Elizabeth"

Elizabeth seemed to possess a charisma that was appreciated by all classes of society. She was able to relate to the wealthy people who surrounded her "without losing the common touch which bound her to her subjects."[15] She appeared to genuinely care for her people, and they loved her in return. Author Elizabeth Burton describes a journey Elizabeth made before she was queen. "At Eton the boys crowded out to see her and all along the way the country-folk rushed out to look at 'my lady Elizabeth' and to make her presents

The Invincible Armada

The Spanish Armada was a fleet of armed ships that attempted to invade England in 1588. Spain had the world's most powerful navy at the time, so the Armada's defeat exhilarated the English. Charles Norman summarizes the event in his biography Christopher Marlowe: the Muse's Darling.

"It came undeclared, but the nation was ready. Great stores of ammunition had been gathered, and the shires of England rang to the clatter of drilling yeomanry. . . . The ships that were her floating defense had been refurbished and rearmed. It was Henry VIII who created England's naval power, and it was fitting that his daughter should prove it.

On July 19, 1588, watchers on the shore beheld the floating city of the Invincible Armada, carack and galleon, galley and pinnace, walloping the water in a vast array, their myriad banners staining the Channel air, their sides studded with guns, their decks thickly clustered by knights and soldiers. Then, after wind, water and fire, and the English valor had beaten them off and scattered their remnants as far as the coast of Ireland, England's exultation blazed forth: bonfires in the streets, beacon fires on the hills, prayers in crowded churches, and the clangor of pealing church bells over all."

Before its defeat in the English Channel, the "invincible" Spanish Armada was the most powerful navy in the world.

of bread, cakes, honey and nosegays plucked from cottage gardens."[16]

As queen, Elizabeth displayed great diplomatic skill and worked hard to bring peace and stability to her people. She could not avoid all rebellions and wars, but she ended a conflict with the king of France that her elder half-sister, Mary, had begun. She peacefully reestablished the Church of England as the state church, while easing many Roman Catholics' fears of persecution by encouraging several Catholic suitors, among them Philip, the king of Spain. Coincidently, this maneuver kept Philip from taking military action against England for many years. When he finally did send his navy, the Spanish Armada, to attack the English fleet in 1588, Elizabeth had had time to build up a navy powerful enough to defeat the Spaniards.

New Prosperity

English life remained difficult and dangerous despite the political stability that Elizabeth brought to her country. Due to her stabilizing influence and an economic upswing, however, the standard of living gradually improved. Cities began to grow. London swelled from a town of fifty thousand in 1520 to a bustling metropolis of over two hundred thousand in 1600. Elizabethan playwright Thomas Dekker describes the scene. (Spelling and punctuation in Dekker's writing and that of his contemporaries in this book have been modernized for ease of reading.)

In every street, carts and coaches make such a thundering as if the world ran upon wheels. At every corner, men, women, and children meet in such shoals that posts are set up . . . to strengthen the houses, lest with jostling one another

Elizabeth brought economic stability to her country. During her reign, a prosperous new middle class arose that included merchants and craftspeople. Bakers, like these from an English guild, prospered during the sixteenth century.

they should shoulder them down. Besides, hammers are beating in one place, tubs hooping in another, pots clinking in a third, water tankards running at a tilt in a fourth. Here are porters sweating under burdens, their merchant's men bearing bags of money. [Peddlers] . . . skip out of one shop into another. Trades-men . . . are lusty at legs [strong] and never stand still.[17]

Miracles and Moralities **19**

An Elizabethan dining scene illustrates the prosperity brought to England during the age of Elizabeth.

Amidst the hustle and bustle, a prosperous new middle class made up of merchants and craftspeople built larger houses, wore finer clothes, and ate better food than ever before. According to historian A. H. Dodd, laborers and their families in the Middle Ages had been "content with 'a good round log for a pillow' and lay on straw pallets with a harsh coverlet of rough-woven yarn or woolen shreds."[18] During Elizabeth's reign, those same people could afford a feather mattress; some even slept on a four-poster bed complete with pillows and coverlets. A few well-to-do families installed an indoor "house of easement" (pit toilet) in their homes. Upper-class women took baths, although not often, in portable tubs placed in front of the bedroom fire.

Despite this new prosperity, a segment of the people still remained miserably poor. As one observer wrote, "Great multitudes of people . . . were brought to inhabit in small rooms [in London], whereof a great part are seen very poor . . . heaped up together . . . with many families of children and servants in one house or small tenement."[19]

To help the most destitute, including children, the elderly, and the sick, Elizabeth supported the passage of what became known as the Poor Laws of 1601. Among other things, these laws ensured that parishes (church districts) provided at least some food and work for those in extreme need. In Norwich, the second largest city in the country, "[homeless] children were placed in charge of 'select women' in each ward who taught

The Poor

Despite improvements in the standard of living, the poor were everywhere in Elizabethan times. Rough tramps roamed the highways, and thousands of families faced starvation when the harvest was bad. The problem was greatest in towns, where slums flourished, and many of the poor turned to crime to survive, as Lacey Baldwin Smith describes in The Horizon Book of the Elizabethan World.

"Beggars were a common sight [in London]; hundreds appeared at one noble funeral hoping for the stipend [money] customarily given to their kind on such occasions. Presumably a goodly proportion of beggars doubled as thieves, for a robber seemed to lurk in every shadow, especially in the slums. Schools for pickpockets and crooked gamblers had more applicants than they could accept. Officials whose duty was to check crime often aided it. . . .

'Proper' citizens reacted in two quite different ways. They passed more laws and harsher ones: some two hundred crimes warranted a death penalty. The severed heads of criminals swayed eerily atop London Bridge as a gruesome reminder of the wages of sin. The other reaction was surprisingly humane: poor laws were passed requiring each parish to provide work for the able-bodied. Hospitals and schools were built for the poor, and shelters opened for the unemployable."

Beggars were a common sight on Elizabethan streets, and many beggars made crime their livelihood.

Elizabeth's love of the theater fueled a nationwide renaissance in drama and the arts.

them their rudiments [the basics of hygiene, manners, work ethic, etc.] and set them to productive tasks by which they could earn sixpence a week."[20]

Royal Support

Elizabeth was concerned for her country and her people, but she also made time for entertainment that was exciting and unusual. Drama was just one of many arts she enjoyed, and with her support and encouragement, members of her court began to try to write plays. As Felix Schelling writes:

Upon the accession of the queen, . . . plays became at once extremely popular. . . . The number of recorded performances at court between 1558 and 1587, including maskings as well as plays, is upwards of two hundred, and it is proba-

ble that no week in any year elapsed without at least one afternoon or evening devoted to this form of amusement. Indeed, no meeting of princes, reception of ambassadors, entertainment, or ceremonial was complete without a play or at least a disguising.[21]

Although ordinary people were not invited to these performances, plenty of actors and budding playwrights were willing to try their hand at writing plays for the general public's entertainment. In addition, a few visionary businessmen saw a chance to make a profit by offering permanent sites where the public could go to watch a play.

The day of the playhouse was at hand. In just a few years, the mobile pageant would give way to the theater. The playhouses of London would draw large crowds of playgoers for decades to come, and would provide the setting for a golden age in drama.

Enter the Playhouse

By Elizabeth's time, plays were a time-honored tradition in England, but the idea of going to the theater to see a play was not. English audiences were used to watching their dramas enacted in churches and on the streets. The nearest approximation to an early playhouse was an arrangement devised for the performance of *The Castle of Perseverance*, a morality play, in which wagon-pageants were moved into a closed circle and surrounded by a ditch to mimic a moated castle setting.

By the late 1500s, however, that tradition had changed. As A. H. Dodd writes, "There remained, however, the problems of the playhouse. . . . Traditional makeshifts [churches or street settings] no longer sufficed; besides, performances were becoming expensive, and the playgoer must be prepared to pay for his fun, which meant shutting out the nonpayer."[22] The solution was to find buildings that were suitable for the performance of plays. By 1600, more than a half dozen London playhouses had established nationwide reputations as homes for the best dramas. The age of the theater had arrived.

The Bear Garden

Historians believe that the concept of permanent structures where audiences could gather first came from the Romans, who built amphitheaters—round or oval arenas surrounded by rising rows of seats—in which spectators could watch animals and gladiators fight each other.

Two structures styled after Roman amphitheaters had been built sometime before 1560 on the south bank of the Thames River in Southwark, a London suburb outside the city limits. Because they were used for animal-baiting events, the buildings were known as the Bull Ring and the Bear Garden. Both were circular wooden arenas, allowing every spectator a good view of the action. Both consisted of a central dirt floor surrounded by roughly built tiers of benches, with thatched roofs over the benches to protect the audience from bad weather.

Although the arenas were located in dangerous neighborhoods, the haunts of criminals and prostitutes, they were extremely popular with ordinary Londoners, who regularly crossed the Thames to watch the animal spectacles.

The Bell, the Crosskeys, and the Bull

Amphitheaters were not the only places where large groups of people came together, however. Over the years, inn courtyards attracted traveling acting companies who realized that the establishments were natural gathering places and thus good locales for a show. At least six inns in London and untold numbers around the country were well known for the plays put on in their yards.

With its circular arena, the Bear Garden gave spectators a good view of the stage, which was used primarily for animal-baiting events.

Felix Schelling mentions three of them: "In a walk northward . . . we should have passed the Bell and the Crosskeys in Gracious Street and the Bull in Bishopsgate Street, all of them inns the yards of which were commonly used for theatrical performances."[23]

In Elizabeth's time, inns were usually multistoried, U-shaped buildings. Some were large and prosperous, others were small and ill kept, but most were built around a central yard, open to the sky. Stages and wagons generally passed through a single entrance into this yard and unloaded their passengers or supplies. Actors who rented an inn (paying the landlord a portion of the money they made during a play's run) did not like the fact that performances were subject to interruption and even cancellation when business at

the inn was brisk. But they appreciated the setting, especially the single entrance, since they could charge a modest fee, known as "gate money," before spectators could get into the yard.

To prepare for a performance, the players first constructed a rough stage made of boards on trestles at one end of the courtyard. The inn's stables, located on the ground floor, were used for dressing rooms. Guest rooms were usually on the upper floors and opened onto a railed balcony overlooking the yard. Space on the balconies was sold to well-to-do patrons, who brought their own chairs or stools and were protected from sun or rain by the overhanging roof. Poor patrons stood in the courtyard to watch the play and coped with the weather as best they could.

The Theatre

When former actor James Burbage decided to build his own public playhouse, he remembered how well the inn-yards served as informal playhouses. He also considered amphitheater design and decided that their circular shape was ideal for seating the large audiences he hoped to attract.

Burbage had been an actor, but he was also a joiner, or carpenter, so he brought necessary skills to the construction of his new building. First, however, he had to overcome two obstacles—a shortage of money and objections from London authorities who did not want playhouses in the city. But Burbage was a stubborn man, and he found solutions to his problems by borrowing money from his brother-in-law and by choosing a building site in the suburb of Shoreditch, outside the city limits.

In 1576, Burbage finished construction on what author Anne Terry White calls "an inn-yard without the inn around it."[24] It was the first of its kind—a building solely for the presentation of plays. Burbage called it The Theatre. It was an immediate success.

No sketch or formal description of The Theatre exists, but most historians agree that it was probably circular. There was a stage set at one end of a roofless arena, where "the actors would get the full light of the open sky . . . and their voices would be heard as though they stood in the very center of a well."[25] The

Elizabethans were a lively people who sought out entertainment. Many people gathered together at inn courtyards, where acting companies performed for the locals.

stage and yard were surrounded by tiers of seats designed to hold an audience of one thousand or more.

Other businessmen were quick to recognize a good idea, and soon built similar public theaters of their own. The next to open, called the Curtain, was built just south of The Theatre. Later came the Rose, built in Southwark near the Bear Garden, and probably drawing its audience from those who enjoyed the animal spectacles. The plays put on at the Rose were full of "battle and bloodshed." As author Martin Holmes writes, "The audience [was] invited to be amazed, alarmed, excited, shocked, or moved with compassion."[26]

The Globe

James Burbage lived long enough to see his son Richard become a famous actor and per-

In addition to his successful acting career, Richard Burbage gained acclaim when he opened the Globe theater.

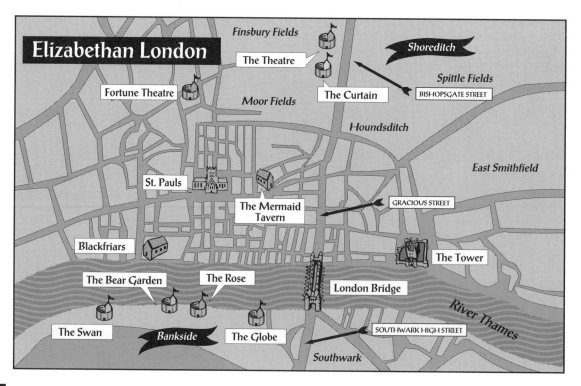

Elizabethan London

Finsbury Fields
The Theatre
Shoreditch
Spittle Fields
Fortune Theatre
Moor Fields
The Curtain
BISHOPSGATE STREET
Houndsditch
East Smithfield
St. Pauls
The Mermaid Tavern
GRACIOUS STREET
Blackfriars
The Tower
The Bear Garden
The Rose
London Bridge
The Swan
Bankside
The Globe
SOUTHWARK HIGH STREET
Southwark
River Thames

Animal baiting was as popular a pastime for Elizabethans as it had been for their ancestors. The English relished blood sport and did not seem to object to cruelty against animals. Even Queen Elizabeth took an interest in this kind of entertainment, and sometimes had suitable animals brought to her palace at Whitehall to perform for her and her court. Historian Ivor Brown describes the gory amusement in Shakespeare in His Time.

"The bears were chained to a long post and then assaulted by mastiffs [dogs]. They fought back under handicap: their teeth had been pared down. But they could still bite and had their claws. The dogs were hurled back and wounded, possibly killed. When a wounded bear was thought to have put up 'a good show' he was released and succeeded by another whose task was to reduce more canine heads to the state of crushed apples. Much the same procedure was followed in the case of the bulls. They could toss instead of claw, and the attendants had an appliance for catching the dogs thus thrown before they crashed to the ground.

Risks were, it is true, sometimes taken by the human agents, but they were only children! Small boys were engaged to chase a blinded bear and whip it into fury; they stood the danger of being mauled if they failed to dodge their blundering victim. . . . It is some comfort to know . . . that at least some of the women [in the audience] were not amused."

Judged by today's standards, animal baiting is a gruesome pastime. Yet hordes of Elizabethans took delight in this blood sport. This sixteenth-century print shows a pack of dogs attacking a bear.

form in many plays in The Theatre. But in 1597 the elder Burbage died. At about the same time, the lease on the land on which The Theatre sat expired. The owner of the land would not renew the lease, so Richard and his brother Cuthbert took matters into their own hands. In the winter of 1598, while the owner was away, they decided to move

the theater, board by board. A description of the scene survives as part of a complaint brought by the angry owner when he returned.

> The said Cuthbert Burbage . . . with the said Richard Burbage and . . . diverse other persons to the number of twelve . . .

(Left) The Globe, perhaps the most famous Elizabethan theater. (Below) William Shakespeare, often described as the most gifted writer of all time, presented many works at the Globe, propelling the theater from obscurity to world renown.

did about the eight and twentieth day of December (1598) . . . riotously assemble themselves together . . . armed with diverse and many unlawful and offensive weapons, as namely swords, daggers, bills [a hook-shaped blade mounted on a staff], axes, and such like. And so armed did then repair unto the said Theatre, and then and there armed as aforesaid in a very riotous, outrageous, and forcible manner, and contrary to the laws of your Highness' realm, attempted to pull down the said Theatre.[27]

The owner lost his case, and the playhouse was rebuilt in Southwark, near the Rose and the Bear Garden. It reopened under a new name—the Globe. Though not the largest theater of its time, the Globe became famous for one reason: William Shakespeare worked and wrote there for most of his career. Many of Shakespeare's greatest works, including *Hamlet*, *Othello*, and *King Lear*, were first presented at the Globe.

This rough sketch of the Swan theater gives historians clues about Elizabethan playhouses, which were usually roofless and multisided. Although not luxurious, these theaters drew large crowds of playgoers.

The Swan

Any detailed plans or drawings of the theaters have been lost in time, although a surviving rough sketch of the Swan theater probably approximates the layout of the others. Historians dispute such missing facts and figures as exact locations and dimensions of the buildings. For instance, some say the largest theaters—probably the Swan and the Fortune—held an audience of perhaps three thousand people, while others believe that the maximum could not have been more than half that.

Despite the debate, most agree that none of the playhouses would be considered luxurious by today's standards. As Felix Schelling remarks, even the best theaters of the era "would have raised in a modern beholder . . . wonder at its small size and disgust at its dinginess and general air of discomfort."[28]

Experts also agree that most of the theaters were many sided and constructed of a timber frame covered with clay plaster or mortar reinforced by sand and horsehair. Roofs were thatched with straw, and atop each was a flagpole. A flag flying above a theater let the public know that a play would be put on that day. The invention of gas or electric lighting was more than two hundred years away, so roofs were open in the center

London was famous for its public theaters, but the city had a few private playhouses as well. These were indoor facilities, patronized by nobility who could afford the higher prices charged to see a performance. The most prestigious was Blackfriars (in reality two theaters), on the north bank of the Thames. Blackfriars' history is described in Hartnoll and Found's Concise Oxford Companion to the Theatre.

"Two Blackfriars theatres were built within the boundaries of the old Blackfriars monastery. The first was used by the Children of the Chapel Royal and of Windsor Chapel [boys' choirs]. . . . It then lapsed and was let out as lodgings. In 1596 James Burbage bought another part for use by the Chamberlain's Men, but was opposed by the authorities, who did not wish to see another playhouse established. In 1600 his son Cuthbert Burbage leased it to the Children of the Chapel [another all-boy company], who played there until 1608, when the Burbages' company, now known as King's Men, appeared there, remaining in possession until the closing of the theatres in 1642.

The second Blackfriars, certainly bigger than the first, . . . [had] galleries on three sides and the stage on the fourth. Its prices were higher than those of the open-air or 'public' theatres. There was no standing room, the pit being filled with benches. Music was a great feature of the house: musicians paid to play there in the hope of attracting patronage from the nobility in the audience. It may have been the first English playhouse to use scenery."

to let in daylight. Candles were used to light the private, indoor Blackfriars theater in London, thus permitting performances in the evening as well as the afternoon, but that feature was an exception, not the rule.

Color and Pageantry

Tiers of wooden seats lined the interior of the typical public theater. A low roof supported by two enormous pillars covered the stage to protect it from rain. A Dutch visitor to the Swan wrote admiringly of these "wooden columns painted in such excellent imitation of marble that it might deceive even the most cunning."[29] The sketch of the Swan shows that these pillars were decorated in classical Greek style with ornamental carving at the top and bottom.

Curtains that draped the stage and the upper balconies also added color and pageantry. As one historian notes, there were several sets of these draperies, which varied to suit the mood of the plays: "For tragic plays, black hangings were usual; comedies, histories or pastoral plays might use red, white or green."[30]

The Stage

The stage itself was usually a rectangular platform that extended into the middle of the auditorium. It was often divided into a front and back portion by a curtain hung upon a rod or wire. The curtain could be opened and closed, thus allowing players on the rear stage to be concealed or revealed to the audience during the performance of a scene. Usually one or more trapdoors were cut in the center of the front stage, through which a player might disappear or leap forth as the action demanded.

A balcony overhanging the rear stage was also considered part of the stage. Players might pretend that this small area was a mountaintop, the battlements of a castle, or a balcony for a lovers' tryst, as they did in Shakespeare's *Romeo and Juliet*. Sometimes a musicians' gallery was tucked behind the balcony. According to *Shakespeare's England*, "Here [the musicians] blew their trumpets to signal the start of battle scenes." Winches, pulleys, ropes, and other pieces of machinery were hidden just above the stage balcony. "Using these devices, the prop man could send stuffed birds or the images of goddesses—even thunderbolts—down to the stage."[31]

The Tiring House

In the wall behind the stage were usually two or more doors that led to an area unseen by the audience, the "tiring house" or "tiring rooms," so named because there the actors attired, or dressed, themselves for the play. Few detailed descriptions of this part of the theater exist, but it had to be a crowded, bustling place.

This sixteenth-century playhouse is typical of an Elizabethan theater.

Individual dressing rooms were not a feature of Elizabethan playhouses, so actors dressed in whatever open space they could commandeer. Trunks of clothing, wigs, and makeup were everywhere. Props and mechanical paraphernalia, necessary for visual or sound effects, were scattered about. Workers were constantly running to and fro. Without electricity, the area was probably rather dim and smoky; windows, candles, and oil lamps would have been the only sources of light.

"A False Wall Fair Painted"

Scenery was not an important part of the Elizabethan stage. The characters and their relationships to one another were the main focus of most plays, and so audiences were content to know a bare minimum about where the action was taking place.

Some settings were communicated by the use of title boards, as historian William Stearns Davis describes: "At one point a change of scene is announced by no more elaborate device than having a boy appear and hang out a large placard [that read] 'A Public Place in Ephesus.'"[32] Simple conventions such as opening or closing the stage curtains cued everyone to a change of scene. Audiences were also aware that curtained-off areas such as the rear of the stage signified an inner room or the inside of a shop.

As time passed, acting companies began to dress up the stage with backdrops of painted canvas stretched on frames. One of these was described as "a false wall fair painted and adorned with stately pillars."[33] Historian Martin Holmes records an instance in which "a painter was paid five shillings for drawing the city and temple of Jerusalem and for painting towers, and the title of the play was set up in ornamental lettering, with the names of the various houses, in red, black and gold at the cost of another shilling."[34] This imaginative backdrop undoubtedly delighted the audience, but it was probably not the norm at the time.

Stage Furniture

Stage furniture, or properties (props), was an important means of keeping an audience in touch with the setting of a play. Every acting company owned several trunkloads of objects that provided realism and interest to what

This view of the Red Bull playhouse includes a rear curtain and stage props, two Elizabethan conventions that made plays more interesting.

would otherwise be a bare stage. These props ranged from a sword or a stool to a dragon, a throne, or a hell-mouth.

When used creatively, a minimum of objects could suggest a complex setting. For instance, audiences knew that tables, benches, and flagons (cups for ale) indicated a tavern. A small forge identified the scene as a blacksmith shop. According to Schelling, "'Books lying confusedly within the curtain' were enough for the study of Horace or Faustus; 'a stool, cushion, looking-glass, chafing dish and a couple of vials of cosmetic' furnished out the lodgings of a lady of pleasure."[35] White draperies, suspended from the ceiling, were used for clouds, and big drums rumbling behind the scenes symbolized a thunderstorm.

The Puritan Influence

Audiences loved the excitement and make-believe of the theater, but some shunned the playhouses and did everything in their power to close them down. Leaders in this opposition were the Puritans, a religious group that held extremely strict views in matters of religion and morality. As Marchette Chute writes in *Shakespeare of London*, "The distinguishing mark of any Puritan was his alarming sense of sin . . . and his waking life was spent in a constant struggle to drown out the temptations of the flesh by hard work and prayers."[36]

The Puritans believed dancing and even music were dangerous pastimes that turned a person's thoughts away from the Bible and spiritual things. Not surprisingly, they judged the plays harshly as well. They denounced "the wickedness of the performance of plays on Sundays and holidays," and considered them profane and frivolous, "recognizing in them neither art, poetry, nor good manners."[37]

The Puritans were not the only ones who disapproved of the theaters; civic leaders disliked them as well. In London in particular, officials worked to keep the playhouses outside the city limits, blaming them for all kinds of social ills.

First, they claimed, the plays encouraged laziness. Most were matinees, performed in the afternoon, so ordinary citizens were tempted to leave their work undone when they wanted to see a play. Next, the plays fostered rowdiness. They packed large crowds of people together in a small space, and, to city authorities, this was asking for trouble. The smallest scuffle could turn into a riot in the blink of an eye.

Fire!

Laziness and rowdiness seemed like trivial problems, however, when officials thought about fires and epidemics.

Fire was always a real danger in all Elizabethan buildings, since they were usually constructed of wood, and oil lamps or candles were used for light. In the theaters, draperies and thatched roofs were tinder dry and burned like torches at the slightest spark. The habit of setting off guns, cannons, and other explosives to add excitement to a performance greatly increased the risk. Such fireworks could and did start blazes, as was the case in the Globe theater in 1613, when a blast of flaming wadding, shot from a cannon, landed on the thatched roof. As C. Walter Hodges describes:

Very soon the whole building was in flames. The fire must have been seen fairly soon, for by good fortune all the audience escaped without injury except for one man who was said to have caught his trousers on fire, but had put out his own flames with a bottle of beer.[38]

No fire exits helped audiences escape. Rather, they had to scramble for safety as best they could, hoping that they would not be knocked down and trampled in the process.

Once an alarm was raised, volunteers began the difficult task of putting out the fire, hampered by "a yard filled with suddenly alarmed men and women and quite possibly dominated by the shrieking of terrified horses in the stables."[39] There were no fire extinguishers and no formal fire departments at the time, so the normal practice was to get leather fire buckets, usually stored at the parish church, fill them with water, and empty them on the blaze.

Volunteers also used long-shafted iron hooks to pull down burning buildings before the fire spread through a neighborhood. City officials constantly feared such a conflagration. As Martin Holmes writes, "A whole street, a whole ward of the city might be consumed, and the most obvious targets for blame would be the authorities who had granted permission for the dangerous entertainment to be given in their area."[40] Such a fiery tragedy did take place in September 1666, when virtually all of London burned after a fire started in a baker's shop and raged out of control for five days.

The bubonic plague swept through Europe and Asia during the Middle Ages. The effects were devastating, and theaters in London remained closed during outbreaks.

Elizabethans' terror of bubonic plague was intensified because they did not know its source. Thus, they took desperate, sometimes bizarre, measures to save their lives, as the editors of Shakespeare's England *explain.*

"The plague that struck London in 1592 was no new terror. It had scourged England periodically for a hundred years. In the Middle Ages it had been known in Europe as the Black Death because the bodies of its victims turned black.

With its crazing fever and racking pain, plague crept in from the wharves and river mouths where goods from foreign ports were unloaded. Rats haunting the ships carried the fleas that spread the infection. But the Elizabethans did not know this. They killed stray dogs, which they thought were disease carriers, and let the fleas continue working their evil.

None of the commonly used medical remedies made of herbs and spices had any effect, so a number of folk cures were attempted. In one of these, live chickens were applied to the patient's swollen flesh in an effort to draw out the disease. One chicken after another was applied like a poultice until each one died. If a chicken did not die, it was assumed—erroneously—that the patient had been purged of the plague. There were few recoveries, however."

Fear of Epidemics

Fire was not the only disaster city authorities feared. An epidemic was an all-too-common occurrence in Elizabethan times. Smallpox, scarlet fever, and tuberculosis were just a few of the diseases that regularly killed thousands of people. Bubonic plague was a recurring nightmare. In the 1300s, one-fourth of the population of Europe had died of the disease. No one understood that rats and fleas were responsible for the plague epidemics that swept the city. Those pests were found everywhere, but city officials knew only that strict quarantine kept the illness rate down, and they closed all gathering places at the first sign of trouble. "Any entertainment that could gather together . . . artisans, apprentices, ostlers, tavern-loafers and the like, jammed shoulder to shoulder with more reputable citizens, was to be suspected, and if possible avoided,"[41] writes Martin Holmes.

With every serious outbreak of plague, the theaters were closed. Then, the players had only one option if they wanted to continue their careers. Together with thousands of other citizens, they left London, since the risk of plague decreased outside of the city. Playwright Thomas Dekker described the frightened flight of those who were trying to escape death. "Away they trudge, thick and threefold, some riding, some on foot, some without boots, some in their slippers."[42]

Acting companies habitually went on tour, traveling about the country putting on performances in towns and villages, not only to escape the plague, but to earn extra money. Eventually, however, most players returned to London, where, depending on talent, luck, and temperament, they made their mark or slipped into poverty and obscurity.

Deciding to become an actor was not difficult in Elizabethan days. Making one's living at it, however, was an entirely different story.

3 Little Better than Vagabonds

Early Elizabethan actors struggled against numerous difficulties to make a living at their profession. Not only were many of them poor and out of work, suspected of being thieves and troublemakers, but they were also legislated against by the government. In 1531 and again in 1547, Parliament passed laws that served to group them with drifters and other unemployed men, in danger of a whipping or forced labor if they could not prove they worked at a regular trade or had a permanent residence.

By the late 1500s, however, the circumstances of many actors were improving. Some of them lived conventional lives with their families and performed for months or years at a time at the same playhouse, going to work in the morning and coming home at night. The secret of their success could be traced to no single factor—the times were right, the queen supported their efforts, and the age of the playhouse had arrived. However, those who succeeded had one significant advantage: a noble patron to support and promote them.

The Noblemen's Players

Patronage of the arts existed long before 1572, but it attained special significance that year when London legislators passed a law stating that only actors who were registered servants of a nobleman could go on tour. This law aimed to eliminate the problem of

The earl of Leicester began a trend when he sponsored an acting company, enabling it to tour the country and perform at different theaters.

vagabonds drifting about the country. Since touring could be an important source of income (and was the only career option during a plague epidemic), members of the earl of Leicester's favorite acting company sent an urgent note to their patron, asking his "license to certify that we are your household servants when we shall have occasion to travel amongst our friends, as we do usually once a year and as other noblemen's players do."[43]

Leicester granted their request, and soon other acting companies sought the advantage of sponsorship by a powerful nobleman. These companies eventually performed and competed with one another in one or more of the London theaters. Among the most illustrious companies were the Earl of Pembroke's Men, who performed at the Curtain theater and later at the Swan; the Admiral's Men (sponsored by the Lord High Admiral of England) at the Rose theater and later at the Fortune; and Lord Chamberlain's Men at James Burbage's Theatre and then at the Globe.

The King's Men

The last company, which included Shakespeare and other notable Elizabethan actors,

had a long and interesting heritage. Despite the fame of its members, the company's patron and its name changed many times over a twenty-five-year period (1588–1603). Felix Schelling explains:

> The company of players to which Shakespeare was affiliated throughout his career, although continuous in its existence, suffered many changes in patronage and title, and was successively known as Lord Strange's, the Earl of Derby's, first and second Lord Hunsdon's, and first and second Lord Chamberlain's company, until it finally passed under the royal patronage and became the King's company with the accession of James in 1603.[44]

Shakespeare gestures to the audience during one of his performances. Shakespeare was a member of Lord Chamberlain's Men.

The company's good fortune was ensured when it came under the sponsorship of Henry Carey, Elizabeth's lord chamberlain, in 1594. Since one of Carey's official functions was to supervise entertainment for the queen, it was natural that the company he sponsored would be particularly favored. After her death in 1603, the company was renamed the King's Men by King James, who was also a play enthusiast, and continued to be the leading acting troupe in England. They were given royal livery—scarlet cloaks and capes—and became officially known as Grooms of the Chamber.

In the winter, the King's Men performed at court and in the private Blackfriars theater in London. In the summer, they continued to

Like his predecessor Elizabeth, King James was a patron of the theater. He renamed Shakespeare's company the King's Men after Elizabeth's death in 1603.

perform at the Globe, as they had since its opening in 1599.

Life on the Road

Despite the advent of patrons and theaters, almost every acting company went on tour every year. Some of the most successful, including Lord Chamberlain's Men, did so either to take a few months' break from the London routine or to escape the epidemics of plague that regularly closed the theaters. Others traveled because they could not find work in London. If they wanted to act, they had no option but to go on the road.

Travel in Elizabethan times was difficult, even dangerous. Roads were rutted, unpaved, dusty in summer and muddy in winter. As author Ivor Brown writes, "In winter a full day's journey would begin and end in the dark and there was a perpetual risk of highway robbery. On sodden roads a well-laden wagon might be bogged down and all travel would be made slow and disagreeable by the usual English rains."[45]

Only the more prosperous actors could afford horses. Those who could not, walked. Cart-horses and wagons were available, but the company used those to carry its trunkloads of costumes and props. At the end of a long, weary day, the players sometimes camped along the road or stopped at an inn where they bought a meal and a bed for a few pennies. If the landlord was friendly, they could be asked to entertain the clients and thus might earn a little extra money.

Making Ends Meet

Most acting troupes were talented groups who earned their success, as *Shakespeare's*

A Great Deal of Talent

Elizabethan actors faced unique performing challenges; they often had to take several roles in the course of a single play. This called for a vast array of skills, some of which are described in Shakespeare's England.

Elizabethan audiences demanded actors who were convincing in their roles. Combat scenes were particularly popular, requiring actors to be agile and surefooted.

"The skills demanded of Elizabethan actors were many. Battles and sieges were popular with audiences, as were duels and murders. An actor had to know how to carry on hand-to-hand combat and how to take violent falls without injuring himself or tearing his costume. And he had to be a superlative swordsman—so proficient that he could convince the audience that he was dueling to the death and not merely trading thrusts with another actor. He also had to be agile and light-footed, with a good sense of rhythm. Many plays had scenes in which the actors had to dance, and some plays were concluded with a dance performed by several members of the company.

An actor had to be articulate and have a rich, expressive voice. He was expected to bring out the poetry in a playwright's lines as well as create a [believable] characterization. And he had to be heard over the hubbub of the groundlings, who, during the less dramatic parts of a play, often ate and drank and chattered among themselves. His voice had to have variety too, for all but the leading actors played more than one part in a production."

England describes: "The touring companies were small, well-practiced groups of six or seven actors each. These men were usually so versatile, and so adept at making quick changes, that they could easily present a play of many characters."[46] But being able to survive on tour meant making enough money to meet expenses, and that could be difficult.

Too often audiences were small, either because the citizens linked the presence of actors with outbreaks of disease and disorder or because a competitive touring group had just passed through the town. Of course, London-based companies on tour had an advantage over lesser-known acting troupes. The Londoners had access to the latest and best-written plays. Their members included the most famous and skilled performers in the country. In addition, they could hire a "crier" to advertise their coming and nail up posters that billed them as being straight from the leading London theaters.

When audiences were small and money was scarce, wages had to be cut. Then some actors took odd jobs to make ends meet. Others borrowed money from an acquaintance. If all else failed, the company would disband and the players would return home. As a letter written by theater owner Philip Henslowe reveals, even renowned companies could suffer this fate. "As for my Lord of Pembroke's

[Men] . . . they are all at home and have been these five or six weeks, for they cannot save their charges with travel, as I hear, and were fain [obliged] to pawn their apparel."[47]

Ten Plays in Twelve Days

London theater companies were spared the endless travel of lesser-known companies, but a London player's life was full of challenges. Foremost was the speed with which plays moved through the theaters. Unlike those in modern times, Elizabethan plays did not "run" for several months. Even the most popular were seen for only three or four weeks at a time. In some cases the turnover would be even more rapid. As historian Elizabeth Burton points out, "During one fortnight in Feb-

The Players' Families

The players' families often faced hardships, although there were some advantages to involvement with theater life. In his book How Shakespeare Spent the Day, *Ivor Brown discusses the pros and cons of being an actor's wife in an era when raising children and even staying alive was much more difficult than it is today.*

"A word of sympathetic appreciation may well go to the wives of [the] actors. They bore and cared for very large families in houses with no conveniences and with all the water to be fetched from the nearest conduit, or bought from the professional water-carriers. . . . They had boy-apprentices on their hands as well as their own numerous children.

Life may have been eased for them by the fact that their husbands were kept out

and about all day by their heavy rota of theatrical labours. The men were away part of the night too when there was need for a late rehearsal or there was a command to give an evening performance. However, domestic 'help' would cost very little and we know that [Edward] Alleyn kept one servant and probably had more than one. But there was constant fear of plague. What happened then? The players, with their livelihood in London suddenly withdrawn, often coped with their loss by going on tour, but they could hardly trail a wife and a quiverful of children along with them as all available transport would be needed for themselves and their costumes, swords, and musical instruments. They were on their rounds with harassing fears about what was going on at home."

A player's schedule was demanding; so many Elizabethans patronized the theater that performances were held almost every afternoon.

ruary the Admiral's men on twelve acting days acted in ten different plays."[48]

To complicate matters, these were not classic or familiar plays, performed by actors who may have studied them for years, as is often the case today. Of course, some popular plays were recycled, but the majority were new productions, straight from the pen of the playwright. Thus, actors started from scratch, first having to read the play, then having to memorize their lines, and then determining how their part would best be performed. The process forced them to learn their roles as quickly as possible to be ready to perform in just a few days' time.

A Day in the Theater

Typically, theaters held performances almost every afternoon. That meant that actors had to rise very early in order to rehearse for several hours. Breakfast was a heavy meal; most Elizabethans started their day with bread, salt herring, cold meat, a thick stew called pottage, and cheese. Tea and coffee were unknown, but alcohol was a popular breakfast beverage. As Burton states, even the queen enjoyed a "manchet (a roll or small loaf of wheat bread), ale, beer, wine and a good pottage, like a farmer's, made of mutton or beef" for breakfast.

After the morning's rehearsal, the players' ate a light dinner—bread, cheese, and ale again—since no one wanted to be overly full during a performance. Elizabethans were familiar with vegetables and fruits including turnips, peas, carrots, apples, and pears, but these were eaten only in season, and not many people had developed a taste for them.

Afternoons were taken up with the performances themselves. A play usually began at two o'clock and ran until four, but some went as late as six o'clock. That left only the evenings for exhausted players to relax, eat supper, and attend to other professional responsibilities, which might include keeping an account of income and expenses, managing correspondence, and so forth. Some companies hired a manager to take over these administrative

Little Better than Vagabonds

Periodically, an acting company was called on to perform at court. Once summoned, the players repaired their costumes and props, polished their weapons and musical instruments, and transported everything to the palace. There they held quick rehearsals, both to ensure the best possible performance and to delete material from the play that might offend a royal audience. Rude jokes or sexual references were not the problem. Rather, as historian Ivor Brown states in his book *How Shakespeare Spent the Day*,

The arrangements were passed on by the Lord Chamberlain to the Master of the Revels, who was responsible for the political seemliness of all plays. Absence of comment on matters of State was necessary to pass this censorship, whose vigilance was keenly directed to political and religious references.

Since the performances took place at ten o'clock or later, the players often did not get home until the early hours of the morning. Getting up several hours later to prepare for the day's performance was exhausting. Still, no actor missed a chance to perform for royalty. As Brown points out,

None would wish to miss a Court appearance, especially as the payment to be shared, ten pounds for the company, was reckoned to be most attractive, apart from the honour of the command.

duties. Then the players had more time to read and evaluate new plays, to interview men who wanted to join the company, and to train young actors in the acting craft.

The Talents of the Actor

Becoming a top-notch actor was not easy. In addition to innate ability, a player had much to learn, and there were no acting schools. New actors sharpened their skills by observing and performing, and by getting help from veteran players who were willing to pass on their technique and their wisdom. As one theater expert writes, "The preparation of the young player meant a steady and strict training by his seniors in . . . the proper carriage [wearing] of unusual costume, singing, instrumental music, stage-fighting, and of course, and most thoroughly, in speech and gesture."[49]

Not only did actors have to master speech and gesture; they had to have strong voices as well. There were no microphones or sound systems in those times, so players needed to speak their lines loudly and clearly enough to reach the most distant member of the audience.

Retentive memories were also a requirement; often, very long parts had to be memorized quickly. This task must have seemed impossible to many novices, and indeed, almost all players forgot their lines at one time or another. Such a lapse was known as "drying up," and actors learned to compensate for it by "thribbling," a colorful term for improvising or making up dialogue. Certain playwrights, notably Shakespeare, strongly disliked thribbling, and some authors even went so far as to threaten an actor's life when he made too many mistakes or substituted his own words too often during a performance.

The Sharers

Inevitably, some players were more experienced and more competent than others, so it was only natural that members of an acting company be ranked and classified in some way. In most theaters, the company was loosely divided into three groups: the sharers, the hired men, and the boys.

The sharers were so called because they had invested some of their own money in the acting company and thus shared the profits. Sharers were often senior players, those who had been with the company for a longer period of time. Because of their experience, they usually decided which plays would be performed and assigned the various roles. Richard Burbage, William Kempe, and William Shakespeare were all sharers in their company, Lord Chamberlain's Men.

Another kind of sharer was the housekeeper, the owner of the playhouse. In some instances, ownership was divided; for example, Shakespeare, Burbage, Kempe, and several other actors were housekeepers of the Globe. In other cases, one housekeeper, who need not be an actor at all, was the sole owner. For instance, Philip Henslowe, owner of the Rose theater, was a businessman who got his start in London by investing his wife's money in various enterprises—pawnbroking, starch manufacturing, and animal baiting, among others. Henslowe's favorite investments were in playhouses, however; in 1587 he built the Rose theater, and in 1600 the Fortune. After that, according to Felix Schelling, "Henslowe managed two or three companies and theaters simultaneously, employing both actors and playwrights at much his own terms."[50]

Henslowe was a shrewd manager, but he treated the actors who worked at his theaters fairly and loaned them money when they were in need (perhaps to ensure their loyalty).

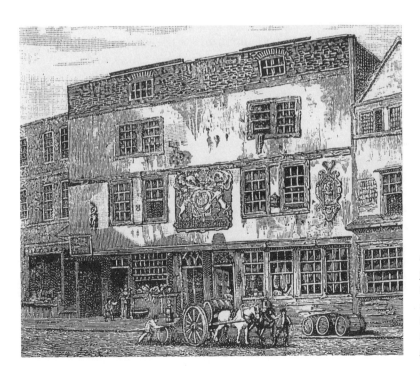

In response to a play-hungry public, businessmen began investing in playhouses. Philip Henslowe grew wealthy through his playhouse investments, including the Fortune theater (pictured).

Little Better than Vagabonds **43**

In a stroke of good fortune, Henslowe went into partnership with actor Edward Alleyn, who had married Henslowe's stepdaughter in 1592. The combination of Alleyn's fame as a leading man and Henslowe's business skills enabled the latter to make an enormous fortune, which he left to his famous son-in-law when he died in 1616.

The Hired Men

A second group of actors, known as hired men, were under the authority of the sharers and housekeepers. The hired men were paid a weekly wage and had no ties to any playhouse. They were hired and fired by the sharers and spent much of their time moving from company to company or theater to theater. Hired men received little of the fame and wealth that went to the most celebrated members of the company, but they were capable actors who commonly took on several parts in a single play.

In addition to their acting responsibilities, some hired men worked as stagehands and performed the daily chores that were part of putting on a play, such as creating sound effects, operating equipment, and managing props. Others served as gatherers, men who stood at the entrance to the theater and the galleries to collect a penny from everyone who entered. Some were tire-men, backstage workers who mended and guarded the players' costumes. Because most garments were expensive, the position of tire-man was considered one of great responsibility at any playhouse.

An even more responsible position was that of book-holder. The book-holder arranged for copies of the original play (the book) to be made so that the players could study it. The book-holder submitted a copy of the play to the Master of the Revels, a government official who licensed and censored plays and supervised the theaters. Most importantly, however, the book-holder stood to one side of the stage during the performance of a play, prompting the actors when they forgot their lines.

The Boys

A third category of players—the boys—was a part of every acting company. Elizabethans accepted the presence of women in their theater audiences, but they would have been scandalized to see women on the stage. As a compromise, female roles were taken by young boys, who, because of their slight figures and high voices, were considered acceptable substitutes.

The practice of using boys in the English theater dates back to the early 1500s, when choirboys sang and performed at court for the king. Eventually such groups were organized into professional acting companies, two of which were known as the Children of the Chapel Royal and the Boys of St. Paul's, named for the churches in which they began singing. For years these boys' companies, under the training and direction of a choirmaster, successfully put on entire plays. According to Schelling, "Of the efficiency of these troupes of youngsters as actors there appears to be no doubt. Some became notable in their day, as did Salathiel Pavy, an actor, strange to say, of old men's parts, who died at the early age of thirteen."[51]

Young males were not restricted to the boys' companies, however. Adult companies soon began using boys to take the female roles in their plays. Youngsters in adult companies were apprenticed to veteran actors who took the responsibility for feeding, housing, and training them. The boys began work at about age ten, learning the correct way to walk and talk onstage. They also studied dancing, singing, and fencing. In addition, every boy was expected to master the tricks of applying feminine makeup and moving gracefully in the many-layered clothing that women wore at the time.

Setbacks and Scandal

The employment of children in adult theater worked well for many years despite a few obvious drawbacks. Inevitably, every boy grew up. His voice would change, and he could no longer convincingly play a female part. When that happened, roles had to be recast with younger actors, and talented adolescents often moved up to become adult players.

Eventually, however, reports of child abuse surfaced, particularly the 1597 case of Nathaniel Giles, manager of the Chapel Children. Giles was charged with kidnapping boys, making them a part of his company, and "compelling them to learn their parts by threat and use of the rod."[52] Concern over possible abuse grew, as did public disapproval of young children's taking part in plays that often contained "adult material." Finally in 1600, Henry Evans, another manager of the Chapel Children, involved the boys in several plays that were politically controversial. Public support for the companies dissolved, and the boys' companies broke up around 1608.

Enough for a Careful Man

Boys played many important female roles in Elizabethan plays—Juliet, Cleopatra, Ophelia—so it is not surprising that young actors could be quite well paid. Records show that a boy apprentice might earn three shillings a week and an established young player fifteen shillings a week, twice the pay of a lower ranked hired man.

In 1597 hired men earned between five and eight shillings a week, about the same as an ordinary craftsman. There are few records of how much money a touring actor might make, but the amount was less than that taken in by actors who worked in the London theaters. Though the pay was relatively low, it was still adequate for a man to live on if he were careful.

Many players were not careful, however. They drifted from job to job, wasted their money on drinking and gambling, and enjoyed life with no thought for tomorrow. As historian E. K. Chambers comments: "Certainly all players did not grow rich, even in London. Some of them to the end, perhaps the majority, remained threadbare companions enough; in and out of debt, spongers upon their fellows, frequenters of pawnshops, acquainted with prison."[53] In Elizabethan times, it was common to be locked up for not paying one's debts.

A Very Good Income

In general, experienced actor-sharers usually earned more than other theater members because of their investment in the company. Records show that a sharer might reasonably hope to earn 100 to 150 pounds a year at a time when 200 pounds was a very good income. Invested wisely, that income allowed a man to marry, purchase a home, and move up the social ladder.

Leading man Richard Burbage and his wife owned a London home that was valuable enough to be robbed in 1615. Shakespeare

This account shows payments to William Shakespeare for court performances. Besides such notable figures as Shakespeare, other actor-sharers and housekeepers also grew wealthy through their theater investments.

was able to purchase one of the largest houses in Stratford, his hometown. Actor Edward Alleyn grew wealthy enough to purchase a manor house and several large tracts of land.

Of course, actor-sharers and housekeepers were always faced with the expenses that came with owning a theater. Taxes, rents, and upkeep of buildings were regular outlays. Salaries for hired men and boys had to be paid. Theater furnishings had to be maintained, and plays had to be purchased.

The last was a considerable expense, as so many plays were put on in the course of a year. An old play—one that had been performed in other theaters—could be purchased for as little as two pounds, but a new one from a popular playwright could cost three times as much.

Rich and Costly Costumes

The purchase of costumes was a significant drain on any company's profits. As Felix Schelling writes: "If the scenes and hangings of the early London playhouses were rude and meager, the costumes of the players were often exceedingly rich and costly."[54] Philip

Troublesome Fashions

Elizabethan costumes were elaborate and eye-catching, but they had their drawbacks, as Marchette Chute explains in Shakespeare of London.

"From the point of view of a costumer, everything about contemporary fashions was designed to give the actors as much trouble, discomfort and expense as possible. The basic idea of Elizabethan tailoring was a smooth, unbroken fit, and the clothes were curved with whalebone or padded with buckram [stiff cloth] to make them stand out from the body. . . . All tailors depended heavily on 'bombast,' which was a stuffing made of cotton or horsehair or even of bran or rags, to give their customers the correct bulges that fashion demanded, and the problem of how to combine this rigid shape with the violent action that was demanded on the stage, especially in duelling scenes, was one that each tailor had to solve for himself.

A quick change of costume could not have been easy, since all the clothes were held on by an intricate system of fastenings. The stocking were fastened to the doublets [jackets] by a series of laces or points. . . . The cloak was held to the shoulders by concealed cords in the lining that were knotted under the armholes, and the jerkins [vests] had extra slits that could be buttoned to ensure a smooth fit. The costumes of the women were even more complicated because of the lavish use of pins. . . . Wire pins cost about a penny a hundred and costumers depended on them heavily, although by great good fortune hooks and eyes were also in general use."

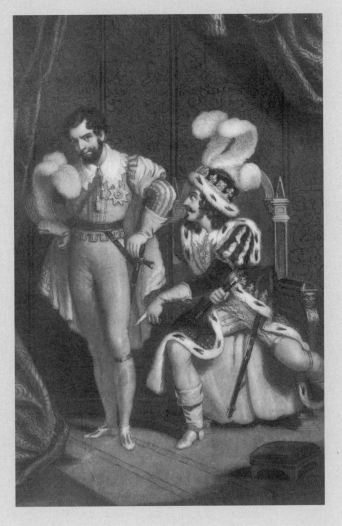

Elaborate Elizabethan fashions were troublesome to change, making costume switches challenging.

Henslowe's records show that a satin doublet cost forty-five shillings, a black velvet gown more than seven pounds. The price of the dress alone would have been the equivalent of more than twenty weeks' salary for one of the hired men.

As theater evolved in London, costumes became richer and more elaborate, often made of costly fabrics such as satin and velvet.

Sometimes tailors were hired to make the costumes from purchased fabric. At other times, the players were lucky enough to find suitable clothing for sale. As one Elizabethan explained, "It is an English custom that when distinguished gentlemen or knights die, almost their best clothes are given to their servants; but they, since it is not fitting that they should wear them, sell them cheaply to actors." [55]

Social Status and Attire

Not only was it "not fitting" that servants should wear their master's clothes, it was against the law. Elizabethans were very conscious of their position in society, and anyone trying to dress above oneself could be punished. Of course, actors were exempt from this regulation, since pretending to be a king or a wealthy nobleman was part of their job. In the end, even if the costumes were expensive, they were judged worth the cost if they improved the play. The better the play, the larger the audience; and the larger the audience, the greater the profit.

Playwrights and playhouse owners never overlooked or took for granted the members of the audience who paid their pennies and crowded into the theaters. Most were ordinary people—craftsmen, scholars, soldiers, and merchants—but their tastes and expectations had to be catered to if the dramas were to remain popular.

This play-hungry public was one of the essential features of the Elizabethan theater, enlivening and stimulating the art just as the theater inspired and delighted them in return.

Groundlings and Six-Penny Gallants

Although most playgoers were crafts-people and merchants, Elizabethan audiences included a cross section of English society: noblemen and their ladies, thieves and prostitutes, visitors from other cities and countries, curious country folk who looked forward to telling their friends and neighbors of their exciting experience when they went home. Playgoing was entertaining and inexpensive, and all most Londoners had to do to see a play was cross to the south bank of the Thames River.

They could make this crossing in one of two ways. First, there was London Bridge, a broadly built span that modern observers might have mistaken for a city street. It was crowded from one end to the other with multistory houses and shops. Only a narrow cobbled street ran down the middle, and that street was always jammed with pedestrians.

The second option was to hire the services of the wherry-men, who, perched in small boats, were always ready to ferry the crowds across the river for a price. Some riders grumbled at the cost of transportation but used the service anyway and, once on the other side, "hurried to pay their money and find their places before the trumpet [that announced the beginning of a performance] sounded."[56]

Playgoers could make their way across the Thames River—and hence to the playhouses—by crossing the bustling London Bridge.

The Wherry-Men

Almost every citizen who did business in London had to cross the Thames River, which cut through the metropolis. As Ivor Brown explains in Shakespeare in His Time, *the wherry-men were one of the most popular means of transportation across the river.*

"Along the banks [of the Thames] clustered the boatmen with their wherries [ferries], clamouring for passengers who wished to cross to and from the numerous landing-stages on either side or to use the river for transport up or down stream. . . . The boatmen had a vigorous spokesman and quite an accomplished writer at the beginning of the seventeenth century in John Taylor, known as 'The Water-Poet'. He stated that two thousand small boats were to be found about London in his time, and that along the whole reach of the river . . . there were forty thousand men earning their living with oar and scull. . . . Their ranks were filled with naval veterans who had sailed against the Armada or on the great voyages to the Indies; these sea-dogs were regarded as some of London's toughest characters and famous for their 'unreverend speech'.

It was fortunate for the wherry-men that the principal places of entertainment, whether providing the gory spectacles of the cockpit and bear-baiting or the gentler arts of the theatre, began to be clustered on the South Bank. . . . It was estimated that three or four thousand people crossed the Thames daily to visit the theatres in Southwark."

Always ready to ferry customers across, wherry-men dot the waters and banks of the Thames River.

Elizabethans enjoy a May Day celebration.

A Cross Section of Society

Of course, not everyone patronized the theaters; perhaps sixty to seventy thousand Londoners never went to see a play. Some stayed away for religious reasons. Some simply did not enjoy the pastime. Many could not afford to leave their work undone while they attended a weekday matinee.

Hundreds of working people did give in to temptation and neglect their jobs, but others did not have to. Visitors and nobility did not have to work; they could attend a play any time they wished. Wealthy merchants and bankers were able to arrange their own schedules and thus could find a few hours to get away to the theater. Young legal students who had no afternoon classes at the Inns of Court were regulars. So were soldiers on furlough, eager for some fun before they returned to their companies.

Even some of the very poor unwisely spent their free time watching a play. One author of the time wrote that the "pinched, needy creatures, that live of alms [charitable donations], with scarce clothes for their backs or food for their bellies, make hard shift that they will see a play, let wife and children beg and languish in penury [poverty]."[57]

An Expression of Elizabethan Taste

An extraordinary appeal drew people of all ages and social ranks to the theaters. That appeal lay in the fact that this pastime was the sum of everything Elizabethans considered interesting and fun.

The English had always loved fairs and festivals. Any occasion was a good excuse for celebration. Religious holidays such as Easter,

Christmas, Whitmonday, and Shrove Tuesday were marked by various rituals and festivities. On May Day, Elizabeth Burton notes, "milkmaids wreathed their pails with flowers and danced in the streets," and Halloween was celebrated as a country fair, complete with mummery and "ducking for apples."[58]

Music played a large part in these events, and even in the home musical instruments were left lying about, to be picked up and played as casually as we might turn on the television. According to Burton:

> After dinner it was quite common for family, guests and servants to get together and sing. In country inns . . . the landlord, guests, the local squire, and yeomen and their families would all get together and spend several hours singing with

such skill and enjoyment that foreigners were astonished.[59]

Elizabethan plays were known for their music and their festive spirit; thus, it was natural to consider them another kind of celebration in the spectrum of festivals and shows the English constantly enjoyed throughout the country.

Laughter and Learning

The Elizabethans were a lively people who loved to laugh, and were fond of wordplay and practical jokes. An observation such as "A cannibal is the lovingest man to his enemy; for willingly no man eats what he loves not"[60] would spark hilarious laughter. A majority of

---

The Inns of Court

Many intelligent and well-to-do Elizabethans were educated at Cambridge or Oxford University, two English institutions famous for their scholarship and culture. But as Lacey Baldwin Smith points out, graduates of a lesser-known, unofficial university in London played a significant role both in governing the country and in supporting the dramatic arts.

"Sixteenth-century England had become 'so litigious a world' [given to lawsuits] that a son possessed of a legal education was almost a necessity for a family with fortune and property. Sons of the wealthy and the wellborn flocked to London to the famous Inns of Court and Inns of Chancery, which together formed an unofficial university for the study of law, 'the third university of England.' Their legal training served not

only their families, it was of inestimable value to England also. Most members of Parliament, major officials, and judges were 'graduates' of the Inns, and Inns of Court men became justices of the peace throughout England. . . .

Life in the Inns was an idyll for the energetic, intelligent men who gathered there. Each Inn, which enclosed a beautiful garden, provided living quarters, a library, and a dining hall for its members, who were in touch not only with life at the law courts, government offices, and Parliament but also with the intellectual life of the city. Elizabethan literature and drama owed a great deal to enthusiastic members of the Inns. Many of the great playwrights were patronized by them, and Shakespeare himself wrote plays for showing in the Inn yards."

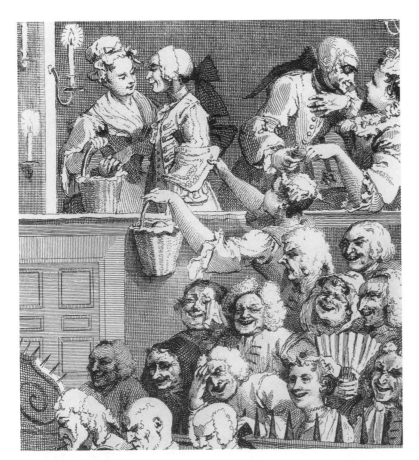

Elizabethans took delight in comedy and loved to laugh.

the plays were comedies, and Elizabethan playwrights made frequent use of humor. Audiences appreciated Shakespeare's offhand puns as much as they did a passionate speech delivered by the foremost tragedian of the time.

At the same time, living in the midst of the Renaissance, Elizabethans were also interested in learning more about the world around them. Improved printing presses were turning out more books than ever before. Travel books, science books, and history books were popular. So were works of fiction, and many people were fascinated by do-it-yourself books on such subjects as beekeeping, dream interpretation, and even turning water into wine.

As the plays dealt with subjects from fantasy to history, Elizabethans satisfied their craving for information by attending the theater as well as reading books. Author Martin Holmes points out: "Londoners . . . came to the theatre prepared not only to enjoy emotional passages and exciting actions, but also to think, and to consider the causes and consequences of the action as well as the deeds themselves."[61]

"Such Toying, Such Smiling, Such Winking"

Elizabethans might have come to the theater prepared to think, but they did not always behave in a thoughtful or dignified manner while they were there. The audiences who paid two and three pennies for seats in the galleries were probably better behaved than the groundlings, those ordinary souls who, for one penny, bought the right to stand on the ground in front of the stage. Nevertheless, there was much laughter, flirting, and fidgeting throughout the theater as everyone tried to get comfortable in cramped and overcrowded surroundings. As Elizabethan writer Stephen Gosson observed in 1579 in *The School of Abuse*:

> In our assemblies at plays in London, you shall see such heaving, and shoving, such itching and shouldering, to sit by women: such care for their garments, that they be not trod on . . . such pillows to their backs, that they get no hurt . . . such giving them pippins [apples] to pass the time . . . such tickling, such toying, such smiling, such winking, and such manning them home . . . that it is a right comedy to mark their behavior.[62]

One historian has calculated that a seat in the galleries would have been limited to a space of about two feet by two feet; not much room for a gentleman's long legs and broad shoulders or a woman's wide skirts. The groundlings were allowed even less room—a space slightly larger than one foot by one foot—and were notorious for their rudeness,

A performance of Shakespeare's Merry Wives of Windsor *at the Globe draws large crowds of playgoers. So many people flocked to the theater that the playhouses could sometimes barely house the large and often unruly crowds.*

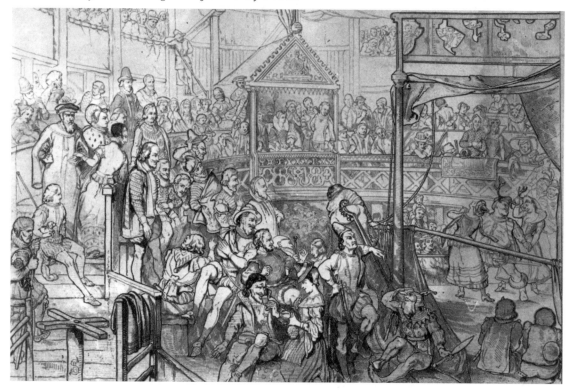

perhaps because they were always being jostled and stepped on.

Once the play began, the playgoers quieted down, and they remained polite and attentive as long as the action and characters held their interest. If the play was boring or the action slow, however, they talked among themselves. During a bad play, the groundlings often became aggressive, as *Shakespeare's England* describes: "Hurling insults and tossing ripe fruit, they drove the actors from the stage. The groundlings, though uneducated, were avid playgoers."[63] They may have been rough and rowdy, but these people formed the bulk of the audience, so they were tolerated by the actors and theater owners for the money they brought in.

Six-Penny Gallants

Theater owners also tolerated the most annoying members of the audience, the "gallants." These were fashionable young men who, for the extravagant price of six pennies, bought the right to sit on stools on the stage during the play. There they talked, played cards and dice, and showed off their expensive clothes without regard for others who could not see or hear. As Thomas Dekker saw it, their attitudes were often deliberately rude and obnoxious:

> If either the company or . . . the weather bind you to sit it out [stay to the end of the play] . . . tickle the earnest ears of your fellow gallants, to make other fools fall a laughing; mew at [make fun of] passionate speeches; . . . find fault with the music; whew at [insult] the children's action; whistle at songs; and, above all, curse the sharers.[64]

Elizabethan women mingle with male audience members during a production at the Globe. Although the presence of females in the audience was frowned upon by some, women were free to attend the theater.

No one knows how the practice of sitting on the stage developed. What is certain is that in the Elizabethan age, as in most eras, the upper classes enjoyed wealth and elevated social position and far more privileges than did working-class people. Certain behavior acceptable for a nobleman would have been totally unacceptable for a member of the general public.

The Gentle Sex

In judging acceptable and unacceptable behavior, some Elizabethans condemned the presence of women in the theater audience. Despite the disapproval, however, a significant

In general, Englishwomen enjoyed greater freedom than did women from other countries. This tavern scene from a 1628 print shows a woman socializing with a group of men.

number of women did attend public plays. As one visitor to London wrote in 1599, "Men and womenfolk visit such places [theaters] without scruple"; another observed in 1614, "These theatres are frequented by a number of respectable and handsome ladies, who come freely and seat themselves among the men without the slightest hesitation."[65]

In fact, Englishwomen had a great deal of freedom compared to women of other countries at this time, and England was called "the paradise of married women." One male visitor to the country recorded these impressions:

> They have the free management of the house or housekeeping. . . . They go to market to buy what they like best to eat. . . . They [pass the time] in walking and riding, in playing at cards or otherwise, in visiting their friends and keeping company, conversing with their equals (whom they term "gossips") and their neighbors, and making merry with them at childbirths, christenings, churchings, and funerals; and all this with the permission and knowledge of their husbands.[66]

Englishwomen were considered the weaker and less intelligent sex, and their options in life were limited, but they were not overprotected or confined to the home. Women of the lower and middle classes often worked as servants or laborers, and most of them reared large families. After a hard day's work, many women visited the neighborhood tavern, alone or with other women friends.

No Place for Children

Women did not take children to taverns, but some undoubtedly took their families with them when they went to the theater. Children did not attend in large numbers, however. Elizabethans tended to see their offspring as miniature grown-ups, and thus did not go out of their way to indulge them with as many treats or entertainments as modern parents might. Instead, most children were kept busy from dawn to dusk, either going to school or helping with endless chores at home. Girls learned to cook, sew, clean, and tend children, and were ready for marriage at sixteen. Boys in the country learned to plow and shoe horses; in cities and towns they became apprentices, working under the close supervision of their masters with seldom an afternoon free for fun.

Even if children had had the time to attend plays, many adults felt that playhouses were no place for children. The dramas often dealt with material that was considered unsuitable for young people. Cost was also a consideration; some parents could scarcely afford an outing to the theater for themselves, let alone for their children, who frequently numbered ten or more.

Temptations to Steal

Mixed in with the respectable playgoers and their families were the undesirables of the audience—petty thieves, beggars, and other dubious characters. As one observer writes, "The galleries were full of light women [prostitutes] who found them a profitable haunt,"[67] and each theater had its share of pickpockets and cutpurses intent on stealing the valuables of unwary playgoers.

In the ranks of the criminals, the pickpocket was of higher status than his associate the cutpurse. A pickpocket relied on the dexterity of his hand and fingers to reach into a pocket and lift a purse or wallet from his victim. The less nimble cutpurse, or "knight of the horn thumb,"[68] depended on his small, sharp knife. With it he could quickly slice through the leather thongs that held a well-filled purse to its owner's belt, catching the thongs between the knife and a large thimble made of animal horn that he wore on his thumb.

All petty thieves were tempted by valuable articles that adorned well-to-do theater patrons. Many wealthy men and women wore jeweled necklaces, earrings, and pins. Their clothes were studded with elaborately carved

Pomanders and Perfume

The well-to-do theatergoer often carried two necessary, but easy-to-steal, items: the pomander and the pouncet box. The pomander was a small, globe-shaped container made of wood or metal. It was punched full of tiny holes, and sometimes was covered with jewels. The pouncet box was a shallow container with a perforated lid. Both items could be made into necklaces or carried in a pocket. Both were designed to be filled with perfumes or spices.

Popular belief held that diseases grew out of foul odors, and many Elizabethans were convinced that illnesses such as the plague could be prevented with perfume. Consequently, people held their pomanders or pouncet boxes to their noses when the bad smells from the streets and from their own unwashed bodies threatened to overcome them. Perfume was also regularly sprinkled throughout homes as well as on clothes and hair.

According to Elizabeth Burton in *The Pageant of Elizabethan England*, "Elizabeth loved perfumes of every kind. She was so delighted with perfumed gloves . . . brought from Italy, that she had a pair trimmed with four roses of silk and had her picture painted wearing them. . . . The Queen, also, had at least one cloak of perfumed Spanish leather and even her shoes were perfumed."

buttons of pearl, gold, and silver. Some carried gold toothpicks with which they conspicuously picked their teeth during the play. All of these items could be easily lost or stolen in the confusion of the crowd.

Even the queen lost valuables—jewels from her dresses, gold and pearl buttons, diamond pins. Author Elizabeth Burton notes, "It is very probable that such things were snipped from her gowns by those who sat next to her at banquets . . . and pageants which were given wherever she went."[69]

Ornate gowns and expensive jewelry, such as Queen Elizabeth wore, made women easy targets for the pickpockets and thieves who preyed on theater audiences.

Although otherwise harmless people might have taken these articles just because they wanted a souvenir of the queen, such incidents still show how easy it was to steal, even from a person who was closely guarded at all times.

Dressed for the Plays

The queen wore gold and diamonds when she watched the plays, but average playgoers were not so extravagantly dressed when they went to the theater. The poorer members of the audience wore homespun garments—dresses, smocks, breeches, and cloaks—of dark color and modest design. Many wore a cloth cap made of wool, in response to a 1571 law making it compulsory for everyone over the age of seven (except the wealthy) to wear such a hat, at least on Sundays. The law was designed both to help the wool trade and to ensure that cap makers kept busy and were not "ranging and gadding through the realm, in practicing and exercising sundry kinds of lewdness."[70] The law was repealed in 1597, but thrifty citizens no doubt continued to wear the serviceable caps for years.

Wealthier theatergoers wore clothing that was brightly colored and highly decorated. Men favored embroidered doublets (jackets), painted gloves, and highly starched white ruffs (large, pleated collars). One of their favorite garments was the cloak, which was often the most valuable article of clothing they owned, sometimes costing hundreds of pounds.

Elizabethan women laced themselves into petticoats and corsets rigidly shaped with "busks" (stays) made of iron, then tied on an overskirt that could be hooped or padded around the hips. Those garments were covered by a kirtle, a one-piece dress, and topped with a loose, sleeveless gown in one of

Elizabethans' teeth were rarely healthy, in part due to their habit of eating sweets. In Elizabeth Burton's Pageant of Elizabethan England, *the author explains other misconceptions that led to dental problems and the lengths to which people went to hide those problems.*

"Teeth . . . did not last, partly because of the quite extraordinary kinds of [tooth powders] used. Some were made of honey and salt burned to ashes; others of powdered rabbit's head, pomegranate peel, and red peach blossom. A favourite was plain sugar and honey. This must have had a lovely, sweet taste and encouraged people to clean their teeth but it undoubtedly contributed to decay. . . . Stubborn stains . . . [were] removed by rubbing with a mixture of powdered pumice, brick and coral. This, in time, removed the enamel as well as the stain. . . .

Yet, after all the washing, drying, and picking, nothing really saved the Elizabethans' teeth—perhaps because of the quantities of sugar they ate. . . . When the condition of the teeth had deteriorated too far, the wretched beauty was advised, "if the teeth are badly eaten away . . . , the best thing is to lisp and simper rather than laugh or smile broadly." This counsel of despair was also enjoined upon those who suffered from unpleasant breath. It is a horrid thought that bad teeth or halitosis may lie behind the Mona Lisa smile."

---

many popular shades—"Drake's colour satin, Lady Blush satin, Gosling colour taffeta, Popinjay blue, and Lusty Gallant."[71]

To finish this ensemble, a woman then added detachable sleeves (green was a favorite color, as the traditional song "Greensleeves" indicates), ruffs that were sometimes so large that special long-handled spoons had to be made so the wearer could eat, and an article called a stomacher, a triangular garment that covered the chest and stomach. Much of this clothing was heavily embroidered and trimmed with lace. Elizabethans loved embroidery and decorated all kinds of items such as night caps, gloves, and even book covers.

Some female theatergoers wore wigs, either to cover their thinning hair (Queen Elizabeth wore one for this reason as she grew older) or because they did not want to take the time to style their hair every day. Wigs were also worn to hide the scarring that sometimes occurred when hair was bleached. Elizabethan women greatly admired gold or red-gold hair, and used caustic solutions such as oil of vitriol or lead, sulphur, and quicklime to achieve that color, sometimes with disastrous effects on the scalp.

Most wigs were made of human hair, although fine silk or gold wire was also used. According to one historian, "Many rich and fashionable women enticed children with a shilling to part with their hair—if it were golden—and there was a brisk trade in hair selling."[72]

Comfits and Tobacco

Even the best dressed and best behaved members of a theater audience thought nothing of eating and drinking during a play. Refreshments such as apples, oranges, nuts, and bottled ale were sold by vendors inside the theaters, much as peanuts and hot dogs are sold at ball games today. People also brought snacks to the plays, including candy in the shape of animals and fruit and sugared flowers such as roses, violets, and marigolds. "Kissing comfits" (perfumed candies to sweeten the breath) were carried in elaborately shaped "comfit boxes" crafted of silver, gold, and alabaster.

Smoking was a popular practice at the theater as well. Tobacco had recently been introduced to the country from the West Indies, and men, women, and even children were becoming chain-smokers. Some people condemned the practice as "loathsome to the age, hateful to the nose, harmful to the brain, and in the black stinking fume thereof nearest resembling the horrible Stygian smoke of the Pit that is bottomless."[73] Supporters, on the other hand, claimed that tobacco was a cure for all kinds of disorders, particularly those of the lungs.

Smoking was so much a part of life that it was sometimes mentioned in the plays. A character in Ben Jonson's play *Cynthia's Revels* says: "Having paid my money at the door, with much ado, here I take my place and sit down: I have my three sorts of tobacco in my pocket and my light by me and thus I begin."[74]

Royal Standards

There is no evidence that Queen Elizabeth smoked while she watched the plays; plentiful evidence confirms, however, that she was an enthusiastic audience member when dramas were performed for her at court. As one scholar writes, "Elizabeth knew a great deal about the theater, and her standards were high. On at least one occasion, she had been known to call out to the actors on stage to speak louder. And when they did not speak up to her complete satisfaction, she moved her chair nearer."[75]

The queen could be bluntly critical, but if a play moved or amused her, she was quick to show her appreciation. As one historian notes: "She let [the players] know when they had pleased her, and they were gratified."[76]

The actors who performed for Elizabeth were some of the very best, men who had reached the peak of their profession. Who were these men, and how did they achieve such fame? Existing records describing them and their careers give only a glimpse of the qualities that made them different from players who were neither as talented nor as fortunate.

CHAPTER 5

Stars of the Stage

Thousands of actors peopled the Elizabethan theater, and many of their names can still be found in histories of the stage. The English had begun keeping records by the 1500s, and many ordinary people were learning to read and write. As Lacey Baldwin Smith writes, "The Elizabethans were nothing if not communicative. The age's abundance of drama, poetry, and fiction attests to that. Along with this, they left behind millions of letters, pamphlets, broadsides, diaries, account books . . . [and] journals."[77]

Yet few accounts chronicle the actors' personal lives. Most were ordinary men whose daily activities went unrecorded by themselves or by historians. In fact, even such basic facts as dates of birth and death have sometimes been lost, as historian E. K. Chambers demonstrates in his 1923 book, *The Elizabethan Stage*. The only information listed in reference to one actor who worked with the Children of the Chapel Royal from 1509 to 1513 reads: "Alderson, William, Chapel, 1509–13." Even when the information is slightly more detailed, the picture is incomplete. For instance, in the case of Richard Juby, one of the Admiral's Men, a short note after his name reads only, "His son Richard was baptized at St. Saviour's, Southward, on 1 May 1602."[78]

In the middle of such dry listings, a few names stand out because they are followed by numerous details. These names usually belong to the stars of the stage, the celebrities who made a lasting mark in the theater. A few of these men are famous for something other than acting. For example, William Shakespeare and Ben Jonson were actors, but they are better known for the plays they wrote. James Burbage began his career as an actor, but gained a place in history for the creation of his playhouse, The Theatre.

Other men won fame for their acting alone. By their ability and the force of their personalities, they grabbed the audience's attention and captured its loyalty. Some were tragedians, who played serious roles that required great insight and emotional complexity. Others were comedians (clowns), who made their audiences laugh instead of cry. The latter group might have come across as harmless buffoons to the casual observer. In reality, however, they could disrupt a play more easily than any other character on the stage.

Song-and-Dance Man

Perhaps the most well known comedian of Elizabethan times was Richard Tarlton (or Tarleton). No one knows exactly when or where he was born, although it was probably in the town of Candover in western England. There, according to one report, he "kept his father's swine . . . until a servant of the Earl of Leicester, struck with his witty replies, brought him to court." Another account says he was "an apprentice in his youth of this honorable city [London]: . . . when he was young he was leaning to the trade . . . [of] waterbearing."[79]

Details regarding the rest of Tarlton's life are equally sketchy. He had a wife, Kate, who was "of light character"[80] (unfaithful) and a son, Philip. At the height of his career, he ran a tavern in Gracechurch Street and a restaurant in Paternoster Row, both in London.

Tarlton was not a well-educated man, but he realized his ability to make people laugh and used it to climb to the top of his profession. He learned to fence and to play musical instruments, two skills that every good actor needed. He learned to read and write, and he wrote several books, including *Tarlton's Toys*, *Tarlton's Tragical Treatises*, and *Tarlton's Devise upon this unlooked for great snow*. In addition, he wrote a play entitled *The Seven Deadly Sins*. Tarlton also had a talent for dancing and specialized in the jig, a kind of song-and-dance act performed at the end of most plays in public theaters. The jig was so notorious for its vulgar words and actions and attracted such unruly crowds that it was banned in 1612 by London officials.

An Unlikely Legend

As a clown, Tarlton preferred making up his own jokes and comedy to following someone else's direction. He pretended to be clumsy and stupid, but with skillful timing he loved to interrupt a scene with funny actions or smart remarks. Some historians believe that Shakespeare, who worked with the comedian and hated to have his plays disrupted, tried to control Tarlton's clowning by writing larger comic roles for him, suggesting as examples Bottom in *A Midsummer Night's Dream* and the first grave digger in *Hamlet*.

No one really knows what Richard Tarlton looked like. The only picture of him is a

The great stars of the theater include Richard Tarlton, whose comic antics appealed to Elizabethans' lively sense of humor.

woodcut drawing printed on the title page of *Tarlton's Jests*, a book written in 1611, long after his death. The drawing shows a short, plump man with a round face, curly hair, and a short mustache and beard. He is wearing the loose-fitting clothes of a rustic, or country person. His cap is shapeless and his short boots are strapped at the ankle. A money bag hangs from his belt and he is playing a pipe and drum. There is no hint in the picture that Tarlton was a legend in his own lifetime and a favorite of the queen.

A Clown at Court

As one of the best comedians in the country, Tarlton was often at court. One historian writes that the queen allowed "Tarleton, a famous comedian, and a pleasant talker . . . , to divert her with stories of the town and the common jests or accidents," but she required that his conversation be "kept within the bounds of modesty and chastity."[81] Unfortunately, Tarlton's humor sometimes went beyond the bounds, especially when he made fun of Elizabeth's favorites, Sir Walter Raleigh or the earl of Leicester. At one time, the queen banished him from the court because of his vulgar and insulting remarks.

Richard Tarlton died in 1588. He was buried at St. Leonard's Church, in Shoreditch, London. His will describes him as an "ordinary groom of her majesties chamber,"[82] a position of honor at that time.

William Kempe (or Kemp), Tarlton's successor, was another of the most popular comedians of the Elizabethan era. His clowning, like Tarlton's, was physical and uncontrolled. He liked to sing and dance, and made people laugh by making funny faces or tossing out clever one-liners. A speech in the anonymous play *The Pilgrimage to Parnassus*, written in 1597, describes his comedic style.

> Clowns have been thrust into plays by head and shoulders ever since Kempe could make a scurvy face. . . . Why, if thou canst but draw thy mouth awry, lay thy leg over thy staff, saw a piece of cheese asunder with a dagger, lap up drink on the earth, I warrant thee they'll laugh mightily.[83]

The date and place of Kempe's birth are unrecorded, and less is known of his appearance and personal life than of Tarlton's. Kempe performed in France, the Netherlands, and Denmark before traveling to England and gaining fame there. The acting companies he joined included Leicester's Men, Strange's Men, and Lord Chamberlain's Men. He was a sharer in the last group

Suppression of Jigs

London audiences enjoyed jigs so much that one concluded almost every play. The bawdy song-and-dance act caused such disorder, however, that in October 1612 city leaders passed "An Order for suppressing of Jigges att the ende of Playes." That order, published in The Elizabethan Stage *by E. K. Chambers, read as follows:*

"Whereas Complaints have been made at this last General Sessions, that by reason of certain lewd Jigs, songs, and dances used and accustomed at the playhouse called the Fortune in Goldinglane, diverse cut-purses and other lewd and ill disposed persons in great multitudes do resort thither at the end of every play, many times causing tumults and outrages whereby His Majesty's peace is often broke and much mischief like to ensure thereby, It was hereupon expressly commanded and ordered . . . That all Actors of every playhouse within this city . . . utterly abolish all Jigs, Rhymes, and Dances after their plays, And not to tolerate, permit, or suffer any of them to be used upon pain of imprisonment."

from 1594–1599, but suddenly left the company in 1600.

Historians speculate that Kempe's departure may have been the result of a disagreement with Shakespeare, who was also a member of the company. According to one theater expert, "[Kempe] had a strain of defiance, and his crowd-grabbing antics, together with a readiness to substitute his own lines for the author's, could annoy his fellow actors."[84]

Despite Kempe's unwillingness to conform, audiences enjoyed seeing him perform in many of Shakespeare's plays. His role as Falstaff, a lying, bragging, hard-drinking soldier with a sense of humor and a love of life, was particularly popular. Playgoers undoubtedly missed him badly when he left the theater.

Although he was a talented comedian, William Kempe was also famous for his dancing, particularly his rendition of the jig. Even more remarkable, however, was his nine-day morris dance, a fast-moving country dance with complicated steps that he performed in 1600. To win a bet, Kempe danced from London to Norwich, a distance of at least a hundred miles. A drawing on a pamphlet he self-published, entitled *Kemp's Nine Days Wonder*, shows him in the ankle bells and ribbons that were part of the costume of a morris dancer.

After this exhausting stunt, Kempe left England again for Europe. He returned in September 1601 and joined another acting company, Worcester's Men, before year's end. There is no recorded date of Kempe's death, but it may have occurred about 1603. His words "I have danced myself out of the world,"[85] spoken earlier in his life, seem a fitting epitaph.

"All That Was Best in English Acting"

Perhaps the most renowned and respected actor of the Elizabethan era was Richard Burbage, younger son of James Burbage and

This drawing from Kemp's Nine Days Wonder *shows the comedian William Kempe dancing the morris.*

Rhetorical Conventions

Rhetoric is the art of using words effectively, and no serious Elizabethan actor could hope to succeed on the stage without mastering the rhetorical conventions, or practices, of the time. These conventions were a complicated mix of speech and action.

Correct speech involved more than saying one's lines loudly and clearly. An actor had to control the intensity and speed of his speech. He had to lay stress on the correct syllables as he recited poetic lines. As B. L. Joseph points out in *Elizabethan Acting*, even the most inexperienced actor had to learn to "pronounce every lesson and each word, audibly, leisurely and distinctly, ever sounding out the last letter."

Rhetoric also included action. An actor had to know precisely how to move his head and how to walk. Hand gestures were important; specific gestures expressed specific emotions. For example, both hands together extended forward indicated submission. A fist with the index finger pointing straight down was a gesture for urging.

As Marchette Chute writes in *Shakespeare of London*, "An Elizabethan audience [was sensitive] to the use of words, trained and alert to catch their exact meaning and full of joy if they were used well." The actors had to work hard at their craft "if the link that was being forged between the emotions of the audience and the action on the stage was not to be broken."

---

one of the actor-sharers of the Globe theater. Richard was born about 1569, so he was almost thirty years old when the Globe was built.

Burbage's acting career probably began early, as his father was an actor and playhouse owner. Richard undoubtedly grew up in the theater, absorbing the techniques and tricks of the trade from watching the players perform. At some point he married, and he and his wife, Winifred, were able to purchase a comfortable home in Halliwell (Holywell) Street in Shoreditch, a suburb of London. Their first child was born (and buried) in 1607, when Burbage was almost forty years old. The couple went on to have seven more children, but only two, Anne and William, lived more than a few years.

Surprisingly, Burbage was not the tall and handsome leading man modern audiences expect. Rather, he was a sturdily built man, described by some as short and fat. A portrait that he may have painted himself (he was a talented artist) shows him to have light hair, a high forehead, and a well-tended beard and mustache.

Despite his unremarkable appearance, Burbage was a fine actor, whose "name long remained synonymous with all that was best in English acting."[86] Historians believe that many of Shakespeare's plays would not have become so famous had Burbage not interpreted and acted the parts so well. He was considered the definitive Hamlet, and was the first to play the leading role in Shakespeare's *Othello*, *King Lear*, and *Richard III*. His acting style was considered "true to life, though he was certainly faithful also to rhetorical conventions."[87]

Burbage was a member of the King's Men until his death in 1619. The earl of Pembroke joined the country in grieving over the great actor's passing. "I being tenderhearted could not endure to see [a play] so soon after the loss of my old acquaintance Burbage." An

Actor Richard Burbage in the role of Hamlet. Burbage was praised for his ability to bring Shakespeare's plays to life on the stage.

epitaph, written by an unknown Elizabethan, memorialized the death of the tragedian in two words—"Exit Burbage."[88]

Alleyn the Gentleman

Edward Alleyn, another tragedian, was a contemporary of Richard Burbage. More is known about Alleyn than almost any other player of the time because of the memoirs he wrote during his lifetime. He was born in the parish of St. Botolph, Bishopsgate, London, on September 1, 1566. Alleyn's father was the owner of an inn and was also, at least at one time, employed as a porter by the queen,

which placed the family one step up the social ladder from the average Londoner. Edward was said to have been "bred a stage player,"[89] probably meaning he acted from a young age, but he was also considered a gentleman at a time when actors were judged members of the working class or lower.

At age sixteen Alleyn joined Worcester's Men, and eventually gained fame for the heroic roles he enacted. Christopher Marlowe wrote some of his plays with Alleyn in mind for the leading role, much as Shakespeare did for Richard Burbage.

Unlike Burbage, Alleyn was a handsome man with dark hair and eyes and a full beard. Like Burbage, however, Alleyn's reputation as an actor was unsurpassed. Just having his name associated with a play could make it successful; Alleyn could always draw a large

Edward Alleyn, a contemporary of Burbage, also earned a reputation as a talented tragedian.

audience, and his talents could improve even a bad play. He is remembered for leading roles in such plays as *Tamburlaine*, *The Jew of Malta*, and *Doctor Faustus*.

Early Retirement

After the breakup of Worcester's Men, Alleyn joined the Admiral's Men in 1592. He did not remain an actor for long after that, however. In that year he married Joan Woodward, Philip Henslowe's stepdaughter, and the two men formed a highly successful business partnership. Alleyn retired from the stage in 1597. After that he helped run the Bear Garden, which Henslowe owned, and invested in construction of the Fortune theater.

With the opening of the Fortune in 1600, Alleyn came out of retirement for a short time at the request of the queen. This stint on the stage lasted only a few years, however,

and he retired a second time about 1604. By then a rich man, he devoted himself full-time to managing his investments and spending his money. He paid ten thousand pounds (an enormous sum at that time) for a mansion in Dulwich. There he also established the College of God's Gift (Dulwich College), which opened in 1617.

In 1623, after the death of his first wife, Edward Alleyn married a second time. He died three years later at the age of sixty. He was remembered fondly by all who knew him as "a friend of persons of honour, and the patron of writers and members of his own former profession."[90]

Following the Stars

As Tarlton, Kempe, Burbage, and Alleyn left the stage, other men stepped up to take their places. One of these players was Robert

"A General and Valuable Counsellor"

John Heminge (sometimes spelled Heming or Hemings) was not one of the great stars of the stage, but he was a talented player who deserves special notice for his faithfulness and fair dealing.

Heminge was an original member of Lord Chamberlain's Men and served for years as the company treasurer. In 1611 he gave up acting to take over all its administrative duties. According to historian Ivor Brown, "Heminge sat at a desk and was a general and valuable counsellor."

Heminge did not achieve glory in front of the audience, but he worked hard and provided a comfortable home in London for his wife and fourteen children. He was

also a respected father figure in his acting company. As Marchette Chute writes, "Heminges was the one to whom other members of the company turned when they were in trouble, and he helped execute their wills and care for their children."

After Shakespeare's death, Heminge and another member of the company, John Condell, worked to collect the playwright's manuscripts for publication. Their unselfish motives were apparent in a letter to the earl of Pembroke and the earl of Montgomery: "We have . . . done an office to the dead, . . . without ambition either of self-profit or fame; only to keep the memory of so worthy a friend and fellow alive."

Armin, who was born about 1568 and died in 1615. The beginnings of his acting career are not recorded, but he may have been apprenticed to a goldsmith, where by chance he attracted the attention of comedian Richard Tarlton. Tarlton somehow recognized Armin's talent and predicted that he would "enjoy my clown's suit after me."[91] Armin did eventually step into Tarlton's and Kempe's shoes. He was a member of the King's Men and a talented and respected comedian. He considered himself a "foolosopher"—a wise fool—rather than a clown.

Actor John Lowin gained fame when he played many of the roles his predecessor Richard Burbage had made popular.

After Richard Burbage's death, actors Joseph Taylor and John Lowin played many of the tragic roles he had made famous. Taylor was born in 1586, Lowin ten years earlier. Both were prominent actors and respected members of the King's Men. Details of Taylor's life are sketchy, although he became Yeoman of the Revels—keeper of the king's clothing—in 1639. Even the date of his death is uncertain, although it was probably in 1652, when he was sixty-six years old.

John Lowin was an actor throughout most of his life, but when civil war broke out in England in 1642, he was running a tavern. The business was not a moneymaking enterprise. As one historian writes, "In his latter days [Lowin] kept an inn (the Three Pigeons) at Brentford, where he died very old . . . and his poverty was as great as his age."[92] Some historians believe John Lowin died in 1659, some as late as 1669. If the latter date is correct, he was ninety-three, an extremely old man in an age when few people lived to be seventy.

The Plays Come Alive

The actors' personalities and talents were as varied as the plays they brought to life. Those plays were passionate and exuberant, tragedies and comedies, stories of wise men and fools, kings and merchants, chronicles of love and tales of betrayal.

The plays were unique expressions of an exceptional period in theater history. As Felix Schelling says, "English drama reached . . . [a] quality of literary excellence unsurpassed in the literature of other ages and countries."[93]

The Many Faces of the Play

Elizabethan plays were indeed passionate and exuberant, and there seemed to be an endless number of them. At the height of theater activity, which coincided with the last years of Elizabeth's life (1590 to 1603), at least four hundred plays were written and staged in private and public theaters throughout London. For a time after her death, the spirit of the theater continued to flourish, and as many plays were performed during the reign of King James I (1603–1625) as were put on during Elizabeth's rule. The total number of plays written between Elizabeth's rise to the throne in 1558 and the closing of the playhouses in 1642 is estimated to be as high as two thousand.

With such a number and variety to choose from, it is no wonder that audiences were enthusiastic about going to the theater. They no longer had to watch well-known and predictable miracle or morality plays whose purpose was to teach or preach. The new plays were pure entertainment, and, "expressed to the full the bewildering complexities of Elizabethan life."[94]

Poetry and Romance

The plays were an expression of Elizabethan interests and outlook, but few audience members took time to analyze what they saw. If they had, they would have discovered that poetry, romance, violence, and satire were recurring elements in most productions.

Elizabethans were a passionate people, and their plays reflected this spirit. Audiences loved the make-believe and drama of theater productions, such as Shakespeare's Hamlet.

Playwrights used prose and poetry in the plays, and Elizabethan audiences enjoyed listening to both. They also enjoyed long, flowery speeches, called soliloquies, which conveyed information to the audience that no other character was meant to hear.

Of course, ordinary conversation outside of the theater was not flowery or poetic. Instead, people joked, discussed, and exchanged information casually, much as we

The Many Faces of the Play

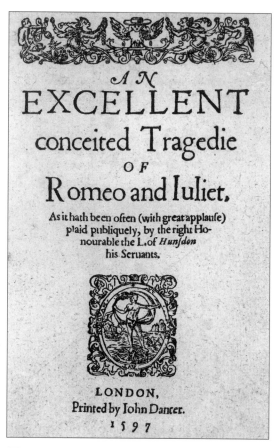

AN
EXCELLENT
conceited Tragedie
OF
Romeo and Iuliet.

As it hath been often (with great applause)
plaid publiquely, by the right Ho-
nourable the L. of *Hunsdon*
his Seruants.

LONDON,
Printed by Iohn Dancer.
1 5 9 7

Theatergoers took delight in tragedy and romance, themes included in Shakespeare's famous Romeo and Juliet.

do today. A letter from a man to his wife demonstrates the normal conversational style:

> Sweetheart, I have received four letters from you. I am glad to hear that you and all my children are well; and for your coming over, I desire it as much as you, and would not have let you have been so long from me, but in respect of your own unfitness to come over, and the hope I had to have gotten ere this into England.[95]

Despite this plain talk, audiences accepted and understood poetic forms of expression, and expected to hear them when they went to the theater.

Elizabethans were very romantic—emotional, idealistic, and sentimental—and the playwrights included plenty of these ingredients in their plays, too. Sometimes, romance was expressed in traditional love stories, in which characters fell in love, killed for love, or suffered and died for love. But romance did not apply only to love and human relationships. Poetry was considered romantic. Adventure and certain kinds of tragedy—shipwrecks, duels, imprisonment—were romantic. So, too, were magic and enchantment.

Certain settings were seen as romantic; many plays were set in faraway lands, which the English imagined to be beautiful and mysterious. Forests, especially enchanted ones, were well suited for romance. In fact, any locale where characters escaped the bustle and hardship of real life could be a romantic setting.

Fairies, Ghosts, and Witches

Fairy tales and ghost stories seem like the essence of romance, enchantment, and mystery today, but in fact, ghosts, witches, and fairies were all too real to Elizabethans, who were highly superstitious people. Their strong beliefs in God and the Bible made it easy for them to believe in unseen forces all around. Many "[lived] in a world that [took] ghosts, fairies, goblins, and fiends entirely for granted."[96] Even royalty was not above such beliefs. Queen Elizabeth had a personal astrologer, Doctor John Dee, whom she consulted as to the best date for her coronation. King James made a study of demonology and believed, to a certain extent, in the black arts.

Because so many people believed in ghosts and goblins, playwrights often included a supernatural element when they wrote their plays. Plays that included a ghost were usually tragedies, and the ghost, usually a victim of murder, was used to spur the main character to action, although some playwrights used ghosts primarily for the thrill they gave the playgoers. Even in Elizabethan times, audiences loved to be scared.

Witches were as fascinating as ghosts, but most playwrights treated them with great respect, probably because witches were thought to be powerful beings who could bring trouble to those who offended them. In addition, real witches seemed to be everywhere. Almost every village had an old woman who could be persuaded to cast a spell to protect cattle from illness or keep one's lover faithful and true. Thus, as Felix Schelling writes:

Heywood, Shakespeare, Middleton, Dekker, and Ford all deal with witchcraft:

King James

James I was less flamboyant than Elizabeth, but his mark in history is nevertheless indelible. In 1611 he sponsored a translation of the Bible, known as the King James Version, that was in standard use by Christians for centuries. His belief in the divine right of kings and his persecution of dissident Puritans contributed to the migration of the Pilgrims to America in 1620. Physically a weak man, James is described by Marchette Chute in Ben Jonson of Westminster.

"James had never had an easy life and in some ways it was surprising that he turned out as well as he did. His father was a weak and vicious fool who was murdered less than two months after James' baptism; his mother was forced to abdicate and he grew up under a succession of regents. His wet nurse was a drunkard and as a result he was so weakened he could not walk until he was six and even then he was condemned to a shamble that for the rest of his life forced him to lean on a courtier or hold a wall for support. If he worked at his desk for a week he became ill, and the only place his ungainly body was really comfortable was on horseback. He could sit a horse for hours without tiring, and his English subjects found they had a king who spent most of his time in the hunting field."

King James succeeded Elizabeth to the throne in 1603. Although historians have described him as a weak man, James played an important role in English history.

imaginatively, realistically, . . . pathetically, in only one case—Heywood's *Wise Woman of Hogsdon*—in the least skeptically. [Ben] Jonson, who repudiated and satirized the followers of alchemy [an early form of chemistry with magical associations] and astrology, hesitated to attack the more terrible superstition of witchcraft.[97]

Fairies were less threatening than witches, since even at their worst they were only mischievous. When Shakespeare presented *A Midsummer Night's Dream*, featuring a fairy king and queen, their attendants, and an elf named Puck, audiences were charmed. Shakespeare's use of fairies "produced a profound impression on the poetic imagination of the day; and thenceforth . . . scenes introducing elves and fairies enter [frequently] . . . into popular plays as well as into performances at court."[98] Playwrights Shakespeare, Thomas Greene, and Ben Jonson included fairies in their productions. Jonson's masque about the fairy prince Oberon was written at the request of King James's son Henry. According to Jonson biographer Marchette Chute, *Oberon* "is one of the most charming shows of his career," with the kingdom of the fairies depicted as "countless lights and colors all shifting, a lovely thing to see."[99]

Poking Fun

Satire was far removed from romance and the supernatural, but this common ingredient of the plays appealed to the Elizabethans' lively sense of humor. Satire, mocking or ridiculing the vices, follies, and stupidities of people, was not new to the theater; it had been part of miracle and morality plays a century before. But in the Elizabethan era, satire

gained new popularity through the talent and boldness of the playwrights. As Schelling writes:

> In the hey-day of . . . Elizabethan drama, no event was too trifling, no personage too august [worthy of respect] to be represented on the stage. . . . Dramatists, courtiers, and even ambassadors were satirized; the citizen was abused and lampooned, or absurdly glorified; the faults, the whims, and the fashions of the day were represented and misrepresented.[100]

A scene from Shakespeare's As You Like It. *Shakespeare included satire and jokes in his dialogue, appealing to Elizabethans' sense of humor.*

Disguise

As Martin Holmes explains in Shakespeare and His Players, *disguise was a popular element of many Elizabethan plays. A person's sex and social class was defined by the clothing he wore; thus a nobleman could camouflage himself simply by throwing on the hooded cloak of a beggar. No matter how much or how little the character changed his appearance, however, other characters in the play were always fooled by the disguise.*

"The Elizabethans . . . liked to see plays about people dressing up and imposing on others who were supposed to be completely taken in by the impersonation. Sometimes their motives were praiseworthy and romantic, at other times—particularly when the author was Ben Jonson—they were reprehensible, extravagant and uproariously funny. The disguise might be necessitated by the course of the plot . . . or the plot might be devised deliberately to display the versatility of the leading actor in a variety of quick changes. In 1596, for instance . . . in *The Blind Beggar of Alexandria* . . . [Edward] Alleyn, starting as a shepherd's son, had occasion to disguise himself successively as a duke, a beggar, a moneylender and a fantastically exaggerated character with an eye-patch, a pistol and a theatrically voluminous cloak."

Using satire, playwrights daringly slipped all kinds of comments on life into their plays. Sometimes these comments took the form of inside jokes, which audiences loved. For instance, in *As You Like It*, Shakespeare described one character as crying "for nothing, like Diana in the fountain."[101] This was a sly reference to a new fountain, shaped like the Roman goddess Diana, that had been built in London about 1595. The fountain had broken down almost immediately, and Shakespeare had taken the opportunity in his play to make fun of incompetent city workers.

Sometimes the comments were critical of the government, the church, or other public figures. In these cases, playwrights usually tried to disguise their criticism by setting their play in an earlier time period, using a false name for the object of their insults, or changing the character in some way. For instance, when Ben Jonson wrote a play that satirized his fellow playwrights John Marston and Thomas Dekker, he named their characters Hedon and Anaides and made one a diplomat, the other an adventurer. Unfortunately, the targets of his insults recognized themselves in spite of his efforts and promptly retaliated (in writing) anyway.

Censorship

Audiences had nothing to fear when they laughed at plays that satirized their world, but playwrights who poked fun at the church, the government, or the crown could face serious consequences. In some cases their plays were censored or banned; in extreme cases both playwright and players were imprisoned. In 1597 *The Isle of Dogs* was judged so offensive and slanderous by London authorities that three actors involved in the performance were thrown into jail. Thomas Nashe, the writer responsible for most of the play, escaped arrest by leaving town. At another time, the Master of Revels in London was so shocked by the players' handling of "matters of divinity and state without judgment or decorum,"[102] that he refused to license any more satirical plays, and performances came to an end for several months.

There were no hard and fast rules to follow when it came to judging whether or not a play might be censored. The Puritans objected to anything having to do with the theater and used any excuse to try to ban a play, no matter what its content. Political figures such as the lord mayor of London wanted to suppress any real or imagined criticism of laws and government. Church leaders wanted to eliminate everything that did not conform to their official doctrine.

Queen Elizabeth and King James were unpredictable. At times they allowed their subjects a great deal of freedom of speech. Such was the case with one play, *A Game at Chess*, which was performed repeatedly in 1624 even though it criticized James's foreign policy. On other issues—references to friends, for instance—they could be merciless. Such was the case when playwrights Ben Jonson and George Chapman were briefly imprisoned in 1605 for including several lines of dialogue insulting to one of the king's Scottish friends in their play *Eastward Ho!*

Bloody Tragedies

In the hands of a skilled playwright, the elements of poetry, romance, the supernatural, and satire could be mixed and remixed to form dozens of distinctive plays. Many of those plays fell into recognizable general categories: tragedies, comedies, and historical dramas were the most popular with theater audiences.

About a third of the plays written at this time were tragedies, those dramas with trag-ic or unhappy endings. Elizabethans enjoyed violent spectacle such as animal baiting, hangings, and public beheadings, so the tragedies often involved bloodshed and death. Still, this type of play could also be romantic and deal with a variety of themes.

Revenge was one of the most popular themes. Used repeatedly by many playwrights, the "intrigue and counter-intrigue between the avenger and his destined victim"[103] could lead to many interesting plot twists that delighted audiences. Moreover, a hot-blooded hero, burning with revenge, was a strong character. So were the villains whose evil ways also stirred up strong emotion in the audience.

Jealousy and ambition were other essential tragic themes that appealed to Elizabethans. Jealous heroes or ambitious villains were fascinating persons, easy to love or hate. They were usually ready for action, and that action could be very violent. In Shakespeare's *Macbeth*, the overwhelming ambition of Macbeth to become king results in both a bloody murder and a terrible revenge. In *Othello*, the noble hero's unreasonable jealousy drives him to murder his wife.

Despite the romantic influence, violence that occurred in the tragedies was not underplayed in any way. Audiences expected to see savage fights, bloody deaths, and gory mutilations. Thus stage props were highly realistic; they could include human skulls, severed arms and legs (made of wood), animal entrails (hearts, liver, and intestines), as well as bags of animal blood. The last could be hidden in an actor's clothing and made to gush forth during a stabbing scene. As author Elizabeth Burton explains, "Realism of a most horrid kind was part of the joy of the Elizabethan theatre. In battles and murders blood and guts liberally strewed the stage—having been procured for the purpose from a local butcher."[104]

A Happy Solution

Although audiences loved tragic performances, comedies were more popular. Playwrights were skilled in finding humorous plots and characters, often adapted from earlier stories written by other authors, just as many of the tragedies were. There were stories about mistaken identity. There were romantic comedies that involved love, rivalry, and trickery. There were the comedies of manners, which dealt with human follies, weaknesses, and foibles.

Comic plots could take endless numbers of twists and turns, but each story always ended on a happy note. This was true of the tragicomedies as well, a mix of tragedy and comedy made popular by Shakespeare. An example of a tragicomedy is *The Merchant of Venice*, in which Shakespeare created a hard-hearted villain, placed his hero in great danger, and then devised an ending to the story that was both believable and upbeat. Tragicomedies were difficult to write because the audience had to be convinced that the happy ending was the logical conclusion for the story. As Felix Schelling writes, "The truest tragicomedy is that which trembles between a tragical and a happy solution." [105]

Historical Dramas

While audiences demanded that the plays be entertaining, they also appreciated historical dramas that satisfied their thirst for

Shakespeare's The Merchant of Venice *delighted audiences with its mix of tragedy and comedy.*

Another scene from The Merchant of Venice. *Shakepeare left an indelible mark in theater with his wildly popular productions.*

information and expressed their newly developed patriotism.

During Elizabeth's reign, a great awakening of national spirit had taken place. Her subjects were proud of their country and embraced books and plays that dealt with English history and English heritage.

Historical dramas, as varied as tragedies and comedies, were based on fact rather than fiction. Shakespeare, for example, regularly consulted Raphael Holinshed's *Chronicles*, a three-volume history of England published in 1587, for his historical dramas *Henry IV* and *Richard III*. The playwrights, however, did not mind embellishing historical events to suit their needs. They sometimes made their characters more colorful and even created imaginary characters in order to please the audience and make the plays more exciting.

Many of the historical dramas revolved around the experiences and exploits of royalty, including several plays written in honor of

Queen Elizabeth after her death. For example, Thomas Heywood's *If You Know Not Me You Know Nobody*, written in 1604, focused on Elizabeth's persecution at the hands of her sister, Mary Tudor. Heywood's play and others served a somewhat unusual purpose, that of memorializing Elizabeth's life and reign. As Schelling explains, "What we should now print as an obituary notice or essay was then dramatized, and furthermore staged."[106]

"The Realm of Mystery and Enchantment"

Historical dramas with foreign settings were as popular as English histories. Some unfolded in France, Spain, Turkey, and Portugal, but a great many took place in Italy.

As the Renaissance, which idealized classical Rome, swept England, the English became fascinated with Italy and adopted bits and pieces of Italian culture. Wealthy homes were decorated with Italian pillars, carvings of Roman gods, and Venetian chests. Many well-to-do English drank out of Venetian glassware and practiced eating with a newfangled Italian invention, the fork. The queen herself was strongly influenced by Italian Renaissance writing and thought. She spoke Italian fluently, sometimes forcing members of her court to speak it as well during negotiations with Italian diplomats.

Of course, most ordinary English people never traveled to Italy, so they depended on their imaginations and the experiences of those who had. "Italy was to the subject of Henry VIII and Elizabeth the land of culture

Audiences' thirst for classical drama made Shakespeare's Julius Caesar, *set in ancient Rome, extremely popular.*

and refinement, and the realm of mystery and enchantment," explains Schelling.[107]

Naturally, plays reflected the Italian influence as well. Some playwrights studied the writings of the ancient Italians, particularly Seneca, a first-century Roman philosopher and playwright. As one historian writes, they "scattered bits of classical lore through their writings like children playing with bits of colored glass. . . . There was hardly a dramatist in London who could resist dragging in references to Hector or Hannibal or Hercules."[108] Others wrote entire plays set in or relating to Italy, including Shakespeare, whose *Julius Caesar* and *Anthony and Cleopatra* both concerned ancient Roman history. Thomas Middleton wrote *Women Beware Women*, a romantic tragedy which focused on a powerful family in Florence. And theater owner Philip Henslowe's records list a number of Italian biographies—*Macchiavelli* and *Cosmo de Medici*, for example—that were performed in his theater.

Plays for Royalty

While ordinary audiences flocked to the tragedies, comedies, and historical dramas that were offered in London's public theaters, noble audiences enjoyed a different kind of entertainment at court. The masque, a simple but elegant type of play, had its roots as far back as the miracle and morality plays, but it reached its height of popularity after Elizabeth's death. During the reign of King James, masques regularly added interest and excitement to palace balls and entertainments.

The masque consisted of an elaborate setting in which players posed, danced, and recited poetic lines of dialogue, "a lyric, scenic, and dramatic framework . . . for a ball,"[109] according to Schelling. Masques were shorter than plays, and they relied on theme rather than plot. Their themes were usually romantic, mythological, and symbolic, involving characters such as wood nymphs, gods, and goddesses, or the personification of such qualities as Love, Pleasure, and Virtue.

A significant difference of masques was that roles were played by the king's noble guests rather than by professional players. And, unlike in ordinary acting companies, women also took part. Costumes were elegant and costly; the more gold, silver, and jewels that glittered in the candlelit halls, the better.

Royal Designers

Playwright Ben Jonson designed most of the masques for King James, coming up with

Royal architect Inigo Jones made plays come alive with his special-effect machinery.

themes, characters, and poetry that pleased even the most critical member of his court. Music was an important part of any masque, just as background music is important in movies today, and Jonson gathered together a great number of instruments and voices to achieve the effects he desired.

Elaborate backdrops, costumes, and props were vital to masques as well, and for those Jonson turned to royal architect Inigo Jones. Jones's talents were as great as Jonson's; the architect invented special-effect machinery that seemed to make clouds drift and ships rock on ocean waves. One masque included giant gold figures of Atlas and Hercules. Jones was a gifted inventor and craftsman, but both he and Jonson were egotistical men, and the two often struggled for supremacy as they went about their business of pleasing the king.

Costly Entertainment

Not surprisingly, all of this glamour and pageantry added up to a great deal of money. Jonson's masque *Love Freed from Ignorance* cost more than seven hundred pounds (of which both he and Inigo Jones each received forty pounds as payment for their services). The masque *Blackness*, in which "the masquers were placed in a great concave shell like mother of pearl, curiously made to move . . . and rise with the billows,"[110] cost more than three thousand pounds. By comparison, Shakespeare spent only sixty pounds to purchase the second-largest house in the town of Stratford in 1597, and a new Globe theater was built and furnished for about fourteen hundred pounds in 1613.

The money for the masques came from the public till. James I did not have a personal fortune—neither did Elizabeth I—and the

Glamour and pageantry were vital to the success of masques, and the public spent huge sums of money on elaborate costumes and props. Pictured are two of Inigo Jones's creations for a masque.

government had no established tax system that kept it well supplied with money. Yet ordinary people were not particularly outraged at the extravagance. The popular philosophy at the time was, "The more money that is spent on things of this sort, the more deserving they [the king or queen] are of praise, for, in truth, they are to be associated with magnanimous princes . . . to whom ugly parsimony [stinginess] is an evil stranger."[111]

For all its glamour and expense, a masque was only a part of a royal evening of entertainment. After the play was enacted, the noble players moved into the ballroom or

A Creative Genius

Inigo Jones was one of the most talented architects and designers of Elizabethan times, but he was also the most temperamental of men. As Marchette Chute writes in Ben Jonson of Westminster, *the relationship between Jones and Jonson was as stormy as it was creative.*

"[Inigo Jones was] born in London, the son of a clothworker in West Smithfield. He . . . had been working at the Danish Court before he came to England to design masques. Nevertheless his heart was . . . in

Italy [where he had been educated]. . . . In time Jones became an architect, one of the greatest in England, and he taught the doctrine of neoclassic Italian architecture as intensely as Jonson tried to teach the precepts of Horace.

Jones and Jonson were rather alike in temperament. They were both brilliant, arrogant, dictatorial men, full of theories and crusading zeal. It is not so remarkable that they finally quarreled as that they worked together in harmony as long as they did.

The chief source of friction between Jones and Jonson was the fact that Jonson considered the script writer the dominant figure in the masque and Jones felt this position belonged to the designer. . . . [They] collaborated on thirteen masques and raised that delicate art to glory between them, but in the end they were not on speaking terms. This was not so much a matter of temperament as a basic difference of opinion, since Jones was trying to build a spectacle and Jonson was trying to create a poem."

A sketch by Inigo Jones shows figures he designed for a royal masque.

the banqueting hall where they enjoyed dinner, dancing, and sometimes more rowdy pleasures. One observer noted the condition of the royal dining room after the masque *Blackness* was performed: "A banquet which was prepared for the king in the great chamber was overturned table and all before it was scarce touched. It were infinite to tell you what losses there were of chains, jewels, purses, and such like loose wear."[112]

Royalty and nobility were not the only ones to enjoy undignified pastimes, however. The playwrights themselves were a rambunctious group, often getting into fights, sometimes landing in prison because of their irresponsible behavior. They were artistic greats, but they were human as well. In the words architect Inigo Jones used to describe Ben Jonson, the playwrights were often "the best of poets but the worst of men."[113]

"This Horde of Writers"

A few Elizabethan playwrights have been singled out for greatness—the most prominent being Christopher Marlowe, William Shakespeare, and Ben Jonson—but there were a host of other men who wrote plays during this era. As Felix Schelling comments, "Turning to the authors of [the dramas], we find at the least two hundred names. The activity of this horde of writers varied from the single play of the gentleman amateur . . . to professionals of . . . surprising activity."[114]

Some were scholars who penned learned university dramas. Some were actor-writers who hurriedly scribbled down their words in the hopes of earning enough money to buy dinner. Some were respectable family men, and others were reckless and irresponsible. Each, however, contributed something to the life and excitement of the theater.

A Hard-Driven Group

Relatively few details about the lives of most Elizabethan playwrights exist, but evidence shows that the majority were a hard-driven group. At any given time, a half dozen or so plays ran in London theaters, most plays for only a short time. Thus, the number of new plays needed was significant. As one historian describes, "More, more, more, was the cry, and there were the wretchedly underpaid quill-pushers, often working in partnerships of two, three or four, to grind the stuff out and meet demand."[115]

To get the plays finished quickly, several playwrights often worked together to come up with ideas, plots, and characters that would please the audience. Usually, a portion of the play was assigned to each writer, who would create his part of the story independently, and then all would come together in the end to fit the pieces together as best they could. Writing at top speed, they managed to produce an average of one new play every two weeks. Sometimes plots were illogical and storylines muddled, but the writers overlooked those shortcomings to get the job done on time.

Scores of writers worked this way. Most took whatever jobs they could, going from one acting company to another, teaming up and splitting apart as soon as their work was done. Working for rival acting companies at rival theaters sometimes created tension when they met in the taverns over an evening's drink. But shared interests led to a feeling of camaraderie between some of them. George Chapman, a writer who worked for Henslowe, was one of Ben Jonson's close associates. Christopher Marlowe and Thomas Kyd, author of a hit play entitled *The Spanish Tragedy*, roomed together at one time. Shakespeare, who did not let his fame go to his head, was friendly with most playwrights, including Ben Jonson, whose critical attitude and bad temper were well known.

Despite all their hard work, most playwrights did not get rich. Shakespeare was one of the few exceptions; he earned as much as two or three hundred pounds a year at the height of his career. Acting companies and theater owners usually paid an average of six to eight pounds for a play, and that amount sometimes had to be divided between several writers. The highest recorded price that Philip Henslowe paid a playwright was twenty pounds to Robert Daborne, a minor dramatist, but that was in 1613 when the price of plays had gone up. As Felix Schelling points out, "The average dramatist of the day could not live on the money return from his plays."[116]

Living Hand-to-Mouth

To help ease their poverty, most took on second jobs such as acting or writing books and pamphlets. Some accepted occasional gifts from noble patrons, although patrons did not regularly pay their troupes of players. Other playwrights lived a hand-to-mouth existence, borrowing and making do with the little that they earned from their plays.

The individual stories of many of these playwrights who worked so hard and earned so little have been lost in time. The names of some men such as Thomas Middleton, John Ford, and John Lyly are remembered, along with the titles of a few of their plays, but details of their lives are sketchy. Playwright Thomas Dekker was a talented and overworked man who spent his life in hopeless poverty, more than once going to prison for debt. George Chapman was so desperate for money that he allegedly wrote a play for a man who wanted to use it to blackmail a woman into marriage. Thomas Heywood is remembered as being the most productive writer of the time, having "either an entire hand or at least a main finger," in more than 220 plays. Many of them were written in taverns, scribbled on tavern bills. Most of Hey-

Rights of Playwrights

Many Elizabethan plays were lost because playwrights saw no point in saving them. As the editors of Shakespeare's England *explain, there were no copyright laws at the time, and even performing a play opened up opportunities for theft from which the playwright had no protection.*

"In selling his work, a writer surrendered all control over it. His play became the property of an acting company. Once performed, however, it could easily be pirated by a publisher or by an actor from a rival company. A man needed only attend the theatre, jot down or memorize the dialogue he heard, and the play was his. Many plays found their way into print by this means. But very often what was printed was a jumbled, corrupt version of the original: the result of bad copying or an actor's poor memory.

Pirated plays, appearing in hastily and badly printed editions, were sold by various booksellers in London, but no matter how many copies were purchased, the playwright was not a single penny richer. When he sold his play, it could be published and resold, and even shortened, without his consent. Material written for the stage was perishable indeed; though this must have angered many playwrights, it did not diminish their efforts."

In addition to well-known Elizabethan playwrights like Christopher Marlowe and William Shakespeare, a score of lesser-known writers wrote for the theater. George Chapman (left) and Thomas Dekker (right) were talented but overworked, earning little for their plays.

wood's plays were performed, but only three were published, and these, according to the author himself, were "corrupt and mangled in their limbs."[117] Heywood may have been referring to the careless way that plays were copied and passed around at the time.

University Wits

Because of their education, Thomas Nashe and Robert Greene stand out from other playwrights who are all but forgotten. Both Greene and Nashe graduated from Cambridge University (Greene went to Oxford as well) and earned the informal title of university wits, probably because of their talent for witty, satirical writing. Nashe was known pri-

marily for his combative nature, the books and pamphlets he wrote, and his play *The Isle of Dogs*, which landed him in trouble with the government. To escape imprisonment, he fled the city, but the incident ended his writing career. The exact date of his death is unknown, but is thought to be before 1601.

Greene became famous not only for the numerous books, pamphlets, and plays he wrote but for the life he led. "He travelled in youth and learnt much wickedness,"[118] writes historian E. K. Chambers. As a young man, Greene married, then deserted his wife and child for the fast life in London. There he took a mistress (the sister of a thief), fathered another child, and began the "penning of plays which was my continual exercise."[119] In 1592, from his deathbed, he wrote a pamphlet

London taverns were popular gathering places in Elizabethan times. Patrons appreciated them not only for their food and drink but for their hospitable atmospheres as Lacey Baldwin Smith describes in The Horizon Book of the Elizabethan World.

"The food in London taverns was not only cheap, it was good, and a wide selection of imported wines was available. There were rooms upstairs for private parties, and diversions of every sort in the taproom. A wonderful din permeated the air: patrons' voices droned; waiters and hostesses shouted to the drawers [bartenders] orders for sack and ale; gamers loudly invoked the services of lady luck; and there was always music in the background. . . .

But the most important element of tavern life was the camaraderie. Tavern habitues formed unofficial clubs; often 'members' simply gathered for a good time, but many taverns became places in which to conduct business or discuss important matters with companions of similar interests. Two neighboring, elegant taverns in Cheapside competed for the patronage of London's brilliant intellectual circle. The Mitre won the devotion of a few of the town's wits; but the Mermaid was more popular. At the Mermaid's tables on any particular evening actors, dramatists, and poets—Shakespeare, Jonson, Donne, Fletcher, Beaumont—might be found drinking, gossiping, and talking shop."

The interior of a sixteenth-century tavern. To the Londoners who frequented them, taverns provided good food, drink, and, most importantly, camaraderie.

An illustration from the title page of a pamphlet written by Robert Greene in 1598. Greene is remembered not only for his witty writing, but also his risqué lifestyle.

entitled *Greene's Groatsworth of Wit*, in which he criticized Shakespeare, whom he believed had stolen the plot of Greene's *Pandosto* for one of his own plays. In the pamphlet, Greene called his contemporary

> an upstart crow, beautified with our feathers, that with his tiger's heart wrapped in a player's hide supposes he is well able to bombast out a blank verse as the best of you. And being an absolute *Johannes fac totum* [Johnny-do-everything], is in his own conceit the only Shake-scene in a country.[120]

The words "tiger's heart wrapped in a player's hide" were a sly modification of a line from Shakespeare's *Henry IV*, "O tiger's heart wrapp'd in a woman's hide!" Ironically, Greene's critical remarks served a purpose he would have regretted. They boosted Lon-

doners' awareness of Shakespeare, who had only started his playwrighting career, and probably furthered the popularity that Greene had envied.

The story goes that Greene died in 1592, after consuming too much wine and pickled herring at a banquet. Some historians believe, however, that he died in the final stage of the venereal disease syphilis.

"Short-Lived Brilliancy"

Another playwright whom Robert Greene criticized and perhaps envied was Christopher Marlowe. Marlowe, another university wit, was born in 1564 in the town of Canterbury, and his career was "of passionate activity, meteoric in its fiery ascent, short-lived brilliancy, and tragical plunge into darkness."[121]

Expected to join the church when he grew up, Marlowe entered Cambridge University in 1580 at age seventeen, and there he began both to write plays and to question his faith. The latter was a dangerous enterprise, since many church and government leaders had become intolerant of anyone who did not support the doctrines of the Church of England. According to historian Charles Norman, "The authorities were going after heresy [religious beliefs opposed to the accepted doctrines of the church] with fire and iron, stake and rack."[122] Disloyalty to the Church of England (of which Queen Elizabeth was the head) was the same as disloyalty to the country itself.

By the time he left Cambridge in 1587, Marlowe knew he wanted to be a writer, not

Christopher Marlowe's brilliant career was cut short when the young playwright was killed during a tavern brawl.

a minister. He moved to London and within the year had written *Tamburlaine*, an epic ten-act drama. *Tamburlaine* proved enormously popular with audiences, and set Marlowe on a path to success. He worked for the Admiral's Men and wrote several plays for Edward Alleyn, who was a member of that company.

Marlowe loved life in London. During the day he often visited the bookstalls of St. Paul's Cathedral, searching for stories that could be successfully dramatized. At night he visited the taverns like so many other actors and playwrights; there he drank, talked shop, and argued with friends.

Marlowe had plenty to argue about. He continued to question his faith, and he constantly blurted out dangerous thoughts. For instance, one night he bragged to friends that "if he were put to write a new Religion, he would undertake both a more Excellent and Admirable method and that all the new testament is filthily written."[123]

It was as if he were looking for trouble. His next play, *The Tragical History of Doctor Faustus*, was the story of a man who sells his soul to the devil in exchange for knowledge, power, and pleasure. The plays that followed, *The Jew of Malta* and *Edward II*, dealt with atheism and homosexuality. All were controversial topics; it was risky business even to talk about such things at the time. Only Marlowe's reputation as a talented playwright kept him from arrest and possible imprisonment.

An Early Death

Unfortunately, Marlowe's recklessness sometimes led to trouble for those who knew him. One friend, Thomas Watson, went to prison after killing a man in a duel that Marlowe had started. Marlowe's former roommate, play-

The Tragicall Hiſtorie of the Life and Death of Doctor Fauſtus.

With new Additions.

Written by Cʜ. Mᴀʀ.

Printed at London for *Iohn Wright*, and are to be ſold at his ſhop without Newgate. 1631.

The title page from Marlowe's controversial play The Tragical History of Doctor Faustus.

wright Thomas Kyd, was imprisoned and tortured after authorities found heretical writing —probably Marlowe's—in Kyd's rooms.

Due to his own reckless lifestyle, Marlowe's own life ended when he was only twenty-nine. On the night of May 30, 1593, he passed an evening with friends in the back room of a tavern. There was an argument and a scuffle. Marlowe was stabbed through the head and died instantly. His career had lasted less than seven years.

Although controversial, Marlowe was so talented that other playwrights, including Shakespeare, were influenced by his style. As Charles Norman writes, "[Marlowe's] work is full of the imagery of a new day—of exploration and discovery in the realms of knowledge. . . . It is an imagery which he helped to shape, and it sheds its light on the pages of the greatest Elizabethans."[124]

A Quarrelsome Man

A great many Elizabethan playwrights—Dekker, Greene, Kyd, and Marlowe to name a few—got into trouble of some sort during their lifetimes. Benjamin Jonson was no exception. Born in 1572 in Westminster, a town just outside of London, Jonson was a bricklayer and a soldier in the army before he decided to become an actor and playwright. His first play, cowritten with Thomas Nashe in 1597, was *The Isle of Dogs*, which landed him and several coactors in jail. The next year Jonson was arrested again, this time for killing a coworker, actor Gabriel Spencer, in a duel.

As if Jonson did not have enough problems, he converted to Catholicism while in prison in 1598, and was soon brought before the Privy Council (high government officials) to answer charges of "popery and treason."[125] He was again imprisoned in 1604, after he angered King James, a Scotsman, with his anti-Scottish comments in the play *Eastward Ho!*

Throughout his life, Jonson annoyed and offended people. He insulted his longtime friend George Chapman, continually downplaying Chapman's talent as a playwright. He criticized Shakespeare's writing style. His competition with royal architect Inigo Jones led the two men to become bitter enemies, while his quick temper and willingness to fight involved him in what became known as the War of the Theaters with John Marston and Thomas Dekker. During the course of the "war," which lasted several years, all three men wrote plays that personally attacked each other. A few years later, however, Jonson

Ben Jonson is considered one of the greatest Elizabethan playwrights, despite his temperamental disposition and reckless lifestyle.

and Marston collaborated on a comedy, and in 1604 Marston dedicated a play "to Benjamin Jonson, that most grave and elegant poet, his very candid and beloved friend."[126]

"O Rare Ben Jonson"

Behind Jonson's quarrelsome manner, "mountain belly and . . . rocky face"[127] dwelt the mind of a brilliant poet and playwright. Early in his life, he had admired the writing styles of classical authors, especially Horace and Cicero, and now he tried to copy their styles. He never mixed comedy and tragedy (something that Shakespeare did constantly) because that was never done in classical drama. Jonson believed that comedy should be realistic; he rejected the fairies or elves Shakespeare used

In Elizabethan times, St. Paul's Cathedral in London was more than a place of worship. It was the center of London society, as Lacey Baldwin Smith explains in The Horizon Book of the Elizabethan World.

"The principal gathering place of all London was St. Paul's Cathedral. People from every social class, from the lord mayor to the poorest apprentice, went there to meet friends, learn the latest gossip, and show off their finery. There were daily sermons, which were well attended if not attended to, for strict concentration was not required; many in the audience walked around and talked until interesting announcements and newssheets were read, or the preacher began a provocative harangue against the government. . . .

The cathedral and its grounds served as a trysting [romantic meeting] place, a park for strolling and chatting, a market for all manner of goods and services. . . . Lawyers assigned themselves pillars where they met their clients, and tombs and the font were used as counters for the sale of groceries and spirits. The largest gallery of bookshops in England lined the churchyard, their names as colorful as their brightly painted signs: the Holy Ghost, the Bishop's Head, the Green Dragon. The view from the church tower was a main tourist attraction, and the tourists were among the chief interests of the cutpurses and thieves who mingled with the crowd."

A horde of Londoners crowds St. Paul's Cathedral and its grounds in this 1620 print.

in *A Midsummer Night's Dream*. And neither should comedy cause loud laughter: As Marchette Chute writes, "Jonson had succeeded in convincing himself that theatregoing was an intellectual exercise in which the rougher and more basic emotions should have no place, and he hoped to find a cultivated audience which would indicate its appreciation with a quiet, inward smile."[128]

Jonson decided that "he would be like one of the great Romans . . . remote, disciplined and calm, and by the force of his example he would rescue the Elizabethan world of letters from its sloppy and emotional ways."[129] Jonson was seldom calm, but his writing was disciplined. Some members of the audience even called it boring. Although his work was criticized by some, one of his earliest plays, *Every Man in His Humour*, turned him into a celebrity, and a later play, *Volpone*, was considered a masterpiece. The characters Jonson created were interesting and realistic, and his talents caught the attention of King James, who soon had Jonson regularly creating masques for performances at court. Jonson continued to write masques for the next twenty-nine years.

The playwright was so self-confident and so proud of his own achievements that in 1616 he compiled a folio, or bound book, of his dramatic and poetic works and paid to have it published. The collection was the first of its kind. His friends and colleagues ridiculed him for the act, but without his commitment, most of his work no doubt would have been lost.

Jonson suffered a severe stroke in 1628, when he was fifty-six. Despite his ill health and increasingly bad temper, his friends remained loyal to him until his death in 1637. The words inscribed on his gravestone express their appreciation of this unique but difficult man: "O rare Ben Jonson."

The Gentle Poet

Many Elizabethan playwrights were unsettled, temperamental men, but William Shakespeare was known for his courtesy and even temper. Born in Stratford in April 1564, he was the third of eight children and probably entered Stratford grammar school when he was seven. There he studied year-round, nine hours a day, until he was twelve or thirteen. There is no evidence that a particular teacher or event sparked his love of writing, but by the time he was twenty-eight Shakespeare had gone to London to seek his fortune; his wife and children remained in Stratford. In 1594 he joined Lord Chamberlain's Men, one

William Shakespeare stands out as one of the most extraordinary writers of all time. His rich and powerful works continue to awe and inspire readers today.

Shakespeare was born in April 1564 in this house in Stratford. Thousands of tourists visit Stratford each year to see this famous birthplace.

of the most popular acting companies in the city, and "the fact that he remained throughout his career a member of a single company, while many other actors and playwrights changed from one to another . . . attests the steadiness of his conduct."[130] Although Shakespeare is remembered for his writing talents, he was for many years an actor, a more prestigious occupation than playwright.

By the end of 1594, at least six of Shakespeare's plays had been successfully performed, and his reputation was growing. Part of his success was sheer genius; he followed the creative drive of his imagination rather than a set of rules as Ben Jonson did. Shakespeare also had the ability to make his stories and his characters come alive. According to one historian, "He read enough for his purposes, he used what he heard in conversation, and he kept his eyes open to the lively spectacle of the boisterous human comedy and of the social and political crises and disasters . . . so amply provided by Elizabethan . . . England."[131]

Last Years of a Genius

From 1594 to 1608, Shakespeare spent all his time in the theater. He was a stockholder in his acting company and part owner of the Globe, and he wrote about two plays a year. *Romeo and Juliet*, *Hamlet*, and *Pericles*, one of Shakespeare's less famous tragedies, were favorites with Elizabethan audiences.

Renamed the King's Men on James I's succession to the throne, Shakespeare's

In the heyday of Elizabethan drama, Shakespeare recites before Queen Elizabeth and her court.

company continued to reign as London's leading theatrical group. According to *Shakespeare's England*, "By this time Shakespeare's reputation had become solidly established in literary circles. The intellectuals were taking his playwriting seriously, and his name was highly regarded at universities, too."[132]

During the last years of his life, Shakespeare divided his time between public life in London and private life in Stratford, where he had family ties and had invested much of his money. Admired for his "civil demeanor, 'his uprightness of dealing,' and '. . . grace in writing,'"[133] he was on good terms with his fellow men to the end of his life.

Shakespeare died in 1616 at age fifty-two and was buried in Stratford. The inscription on his gravestone, which Shakespeare may have written himself, reads:

> Good friend, for Jesus' sake forbear,
> To dig the dust enclosed here;
> Blest be the man that spares these
>   stones,
> And curst be he that moves my bones.[134]

Anti-Stratfordians

As time passed, and increasing numbers of people came to admire Shakespeare's plays for their literary beauty and sophistication, some began to ask how one man—especially a country boy with only a grammar school education—could possibly have produced such a body of work. They argued that Shakespeare did not have the intelligence or the knowledge of the world to write such complex plays. These people, known as the anti-Stratfordians, believed that some other person was the actual author of some of Shakespeare's plays.

Sir Francis Bacon was a popular candidate. Bacon was a philosopher, statesman, and author. He had attended Cambridge University, been an ambassador to France, and served in Parliament. He was certainly sophisticated enough to have written such powerful tragedies as *King Lear* and *Macbeth*.

Several noblemen were also candidates—Edward de Vere, the 17th earl of Oxford; Roger Manners, the 5th earl of Rutland; and William Stanley, the 6th earl of Derby. And there was Sir Walter Raleigh, soldier, writer, and Oxford University graduate. A few anti-Stratfordians even believed that they detected Christopher Marlowe's style in some of the plays; indeed, Shakespeare imitated Marlowe for a time.

Most Shakespearean scholars refute the anti-Stratfordians' arguments, however. They point out that education and travel were not essential for writing great plays. Ben Jonson had only a limited education and began his life as a bricklayer, yet he composed highly sophisticated plays. Scholars also point out that whereas there is no hard evidence to prove that someone else wrote the plays, there is much written proof that supports Shakespeare's authorship. As author Frank Ernest Hill writes, anyone who investigates the question "will find that increasing

Marlowe's Death

Numerous rumors about the circumstances of Christopher Marlowe's death circulated around London in the years after he died. The exact details of his tragic end have been lost in time, but this account, given by eyewitness Ingram Frizer, is recorded in Charles Norman's Christopher Marlowe.

"After supper the said Ingram & Christopher Morley [Marlowe] were in speech & uttered one to the other . . . malicious words for the reason that they could not be at one nor agree about the payment of the sum of pence [their bill] . . . & the said Christopher Morley then lying upon a bed in the room where they supped, & moved with anger against the said Ingram ffrysar [Frizer] . . . And the said Ingram then and there sitting . . . with his back towards the bed where the said Christopher Morley was then lying, . . . it so befell that the said Christopher Morley . . . maliciously drew the dagger of the said Ingram which was at his back, and with the same dagger the said Christopher Morley then & there maliciously gave the aforesaid Ingram two wounds on his head of the length of two inches & of the depth of a quarter of an inch; whereupon the said Ingram, in fear of being slain . . . struggled with the said Christopher Morley to get back from him his dagger . . . and so it befell in that affray that the said Ingram, in defence of his life . . . gave the said Christopher . . . a mortal wound over his right eye of the depth of two inches & of the width of one inch; of which mortal wound the aforesaid Christopher Morley then & there instantly died."

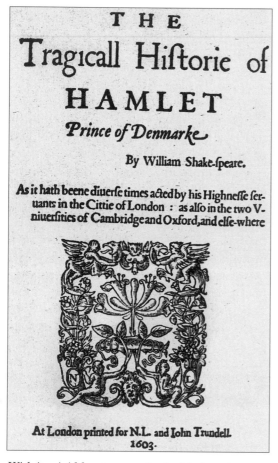

THE
Tragicall Hiſtorie of
HAMLET
Prince of Denmarke

By William Shake-ſpeare.

As it hath beene diuerſe times acted by his Highneſſe ſer-
uants in the Cittie of London : as alſo in the two V-
niuerſities of Cambridge and Oxford, and elſe-where

At London printed for N.L. and Iohn Trundell.
1603.

*With its vivid language and colorful characters,
Shakespeare's* Hamlet *was popular with
Elizabethan audiences.*

knowledge only confirms . . . the reality of
William Shakespeare as actor, playhouse owner, gentleman, and most gifted of writers." [135]

The First Folio

Some of the strongest evidence that Shakespeare wrote his plays lies in the actions of
two of his friends shortly after his death.

Shakespeare did not have Ben Jonson's
ego; he had not given a thought to what would
happen to his plays over time. During the
course of his life, many of the original manuscripts had been lost, although some quartos,
small volumes containing one play, had been
printed. These unauthorized copies were
often inaccurate versions that were scribbled
down by "play pirates" during a performance.
In addition, Shakespeare's plays underwent
constant minor changes by actors and direc-
tors every time they were performed.

Afraid that their friend's work would soon
be significantly altered or even lost, two members of the King's Men, actors John Heminge
and Henry Condell, took on the responsibility of gathering and preserving Shakespeare's
work. Both men had worked with him, so they
could rely on their memories as to what had
originally been written. They also relied on
Shakespeare's notes and prompter's versions
when putting together their finished product.

It was expensive to print plays in folio
form, and many printers hesitated to take the
job for fear they would never be paid. But
after much time and effort, Heminge and
Condell completed their task. On November
8, 1623, seven years after Shakespeare died,
the First Folio appeared. It contained thirty-
six plays in more than nine hundred pages.
The words of Ben Jonson, written in praise of
his friend, appear as a dedication. Those
words have been echoed by generations of
playgoers and Shakespeare enthusiasts:

> Soul of the age!
> The applause! delight! the wonder of our
>   stage!
> My Shakespeare, rise. . . .
> He was not of an age, but for all time. [136]

The Elizabethan Heritage

The death of Shakespeare in 1616 signaled the decline of the Elizabethan theater. The great stars of the stage, Tarlton, Kempe, Burbage, and Alleyn, were dead or nearing the end of their lives. Playwright Ben Jonson was still writing, but Christopher Marlowe, Robert Greene, and many of their contemporaries were gone.

Elizabeth's death in 1603 marked the end of the era that bore her name. Her successor, James I, lacked the diplomacy and personal charisma that had made her popular and successful. By the end of his reign, the country was in an economic downturn, and the numbers of playgoers had decreased due to the influence of the Puritans. Many serious-

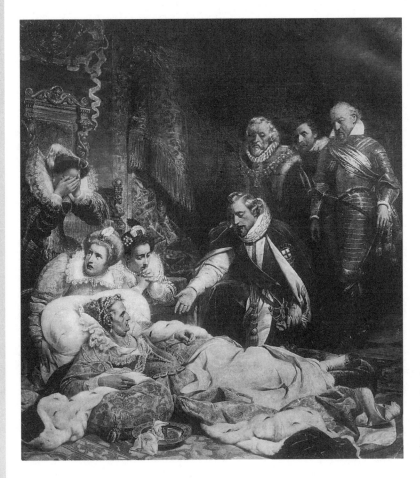

The death of Queen Elizabeth marked the end of a unique era. Despite the decline of the theater shortly after her death, playgoers worldwide inherited a rich body of literature.

minded Londoners objected to having theaters with noisy crowds and the threat of fire and disease in their neighborhood. The scandal-ridden boys' companies had been disbanded. The playhouses were falling into disrepair.

James died in 1625, and his son, Charles I, took the throne. Under Charles, civil war broke out in 1642, and Parliament closed the theaters permanently. Because royalty had supported the theater since before Elizabeth's time, many actors joined the army and fought for the king. Their efforts and those of other loyalists could not reverse the tide of revolutionary sentiment that peaked in 1649. In that year, the Puritans under Oliver Cromwell seized control of the government, beheaded the king, and declared England a republic. The Elizabethan age, like the Elizabethan stage, was no more.

Undying Contributions

But the country's fascination with the theater did not die. By 1660 the people rebelled against Puritan rule, and Parliament restored the monarchy under Charles II. Soon after that, Charles lifted the ban on playgoing, and the theaters reopened.

All was not the same as it had been before the war, however. Many old run-down playhouses were replaced by new indoor theaters. The cost of admission increased to the point that members of the lower class could no longer afford to attend. Inside the theaters, painted backdrops decorated almost every stage, and women were allowed to act.

Despite the changes and adaptations, however, the contributions of the Elizabethan era were not lost. The basic design of the playhouse, pioneered by James Burbage, continued to be used over time. Even today,

galleries of seats curve around a central stage, sets are moveable, dressing rooms are backstage, and musicians are tucked out of sight.

Certain theatrical terms coined by Elizabethans are still in use today. For instance, the box office, the place where tickets are sold, was named for the box into which Elizabethan audiences dropped their pennies when they entered the theater. When actors are said to be "on the boards," or "treading the boards," the reference is to the early stage, which was made of planks and trestles. As Ivor Brown points out, "Much of our theatrical vocabulary has remained unchanged since Shakespeare's time. The prompter still 'holds the book', parts are 'studied' by the actor, [and] the entrances to cheap seats are 'the doors.'"[137]

Not only specialized vocabulary but the English language in general has been influenced and enriched by the Elizabethan theater. Shakespeare in particular was highly talented in putting words together and was not afraid to experiment with vocabulary. He created the phrases "fair play," "catch cold," and "disgraceful conduct," and invented words such as "assassination," "bump," "eventful," and "lonely." Whole lines from his plays are familiar to most modern English speakers. Such lines as "To be or not to be" from *Hamlet* and "One that loved not wisely, but too well" from *Othello* have been quoted (and misquoted) on television and in newspapers and movies for generations.

Influence on Culture

The contributions of the Elizabethans include more than theater design or vocabulary, however. Over time, the plays—especially Shakespeare's—have had an enormous and lasting influence on world culture. They have challenged modern poets and playwrights to experiment with their writing

Eventually, the Puritans gained enough power to discourage theatergoing and finally close the theaters. Felix Schelling describes the legal actions taken against the players and the playhouses in his book Elizabethan Drama.

"The Puritan spirit of the Parliaments of King Charles is patent in a statute of the very first year of his reign which forbids 'the acting of interludes and common plays on Sunday.' In the following year, 1626, a petition for the building of an amphitheater in Lincoln's Inn Fields failed when it was discovered that theatrical performances were to be given therein. . . .

In 1631 the Puritans had become bolder, and a petition was presented to the Bishop of London by the inhabitants of Blackfriars demanding the removal of the playhouse there. . . . At length, in September, 1642, came the ordinance of the Lords and Commons, putting a cease to the performance of all plays on account of the civil war; and several further ordinances were passed to complete the suppression.

The final one of February, 1647, declared all players rogues within the meaning of the old statutes of Elizabeth and James, authorized the mayor, justices, and sheriffs to dismantle all playhouses, assigned whipping as the punishment for an actor caught pursuing his calling, fined each spectator five shillings, and turned over the door money to the relief of the poor."

styles, just as Elizabethan playwrights did. They have provided patterns for artists in related art forms to follow: Successful operas and musicals, such as Verdi's *Otello* and Leonard Bernstein's *West Side Story*, have been based on Elizabethan originals.

Scholars and educators have also come to see the plays as an important part of a good education. In the United States, many students get their first introduction to the theater by studying a Shakespearean play in English class. Worldwide, the plays are read for their historic content, dramatic style, literary beauty, and timeless characters. From them, students learn about cultural, social, and political conditions during the Elizabethan era. They are exposed to fundamental themes of literature such as tragedy, romantic love, and heroism. They gain insight into historical characters in a way that is often more interesting than reading a history book.

Generations of Actors

If ordinary people have been entertained and educated by Shakespearean drama, generations of serious actors consider Shakespearean roles to be the ultimate test of their talent. Great actors of every age—David Garrick, Edmund Kean, Peggy Ashcroft, Laurence Olivier, Richard Burton, and more—made their reputations by portraying Shakespearean characters. Most of these actors were English, but one American—Edwin Booth, brother of Lincoln assassin John Wilkes Booth—was renowned as the finest Shakespearean actor of the late 1800s.

The number of Shakespearean acting companies and theater productions that exist today also bears witness to the continuing importance of Elizabethan drama, both to those involved in the theater and to ordinary people who enjoy watching the plays. In

Sir Laurence Olivier, born in England in 1907, is considered by many to be the greatest Shakespearean actor of modern times. During the course of his career, he played leading roles in Julius Caesar, Othello, Richard III, *and* Hamlet, *which Olivier considered Shakespeare's masterpiece. In his book* On Acting, *Olivier explains why the tragic drama continues to fascinate him after so many years.*

"Hamlet is pound for pound, in my opinion, the greatest play ever written. It towers above everything else in dramatic literature. It gives us great climaxes, shadows and shades, yet contains occasional moments of high comedy. Every time you read a line it can be a new discovery. You can play it and play it as many times as the opportunity occurs and still not get to the bottom of its box of wonders. It can trick you round false corners and into culs-de-sac, or take you by the seat of your pants and hurl you across the stars. It can give you moments of unknown joy, or cast you into the depths of despair. Once you have played it, it will devour you and obsess you for the rest of your life. It has me. I think each day about it. I'll never play him [Hamlet] again, of course, but by God, I wish I could."

Laurence Olivier plays Shakespeare's Hamlet, *which he considered "the greatest play ever written."*

England, the Royal Shakespeare Company regularly performs in London and Stratford. In Canada, a Shakespeare festival takes place annually in Stratford, Ontario. In the United States, festivals from San Diego, California, to Ashland, Oregon, to New York City present Shakespeare every summer.

"The World as It Is"

The legacy of the Elizabethan theater also includes the spirit of the Elizabethans themselves. That spirit encompasses the confidence and daring of the queen who led her

Laurence Olivier plays the leading role in Shakespeare's Richard III. *Elizabethan theater has proved timeless in its appeal.*

nation into a golden age. It also includes the vitality and curiosity of all who created, enacted, and watched the plays. Their energy still motivates drama and the theater today. It touches ordinary people, who catch the excitement when they go to see a play.

The Elizabethan theater expressed the culture of a unique period of history. Some considered it vulgar and unpolished; others found it eloquent and inspired. Both views may have been true, but the content and artistry of its dramas have proved timeless. Just as the Elizabethans were able to learn about other places and other times when they went to the plays, we are able to get a glimpse of another world when we study the work they left behind. Just as they were able to identify with the characters and the problems found in the plays, we too can see our own conflicts and values reflected there.

In the words of Felix Schelling, "Elizabethan drama . . . possesses, as few literatures have ever possessed, the power to disclose the world as it is."[138] When that world is revealed, and we compare ourselves with the Elizabethans—our interests, our priorities, what makes us laugh, and what makes us cry—we discover that we are not so different from them after all.

Notes

Introduction: "A Great National Utterance"

1. William Stearns Davis, *Life in Elizabethan Days*. New York: Harper & Brothers, 1930, p. 5.
2. Quoted in Felix Schelling, *Elizabethan Drama 1558–1642*, vol. 1. Boston: Houghton Mifflin, 1908, p. 149.
3. Quoted in Horizon Magazine, ed., *Shakespeare's England*. New York: American Heritage, 1964, p. 91.
4. Schelling, *Elizabethan Drama*, vol. 1, p. xlii.

Chapter 1: Miracles and Moralities

5. Quoted in Ivor Brown, *How Shakespeare Spent the Day*. New York: Hill & Wang, 1963, p. 196.
6. Schelling, *Elizabethan Drama*, vol. 1, p. xxiii.
7. C. Walter Hodges, *Shakespeare's Theatre*. New York: Coward-McCann, 1964, p. 14.
8. Davis, *Life In Elizabethan Days*, p. 114.
9. Hodges, *Shakespeare's Theatre*, p. 22.
10. Schelling, *Elizabethan Drama*, vol. 1, p. 24.
11. Hodges, *Shakespeare's Theatre*, p. 32.
12. Quoted in Schelling, *Elizabethan Drama*, vol. 1, p. 24.
13. Schelling, *Elizabethan Drama*, vol. 1, p. 185.
14. A. H. Dodd, *Elizabethan England*. London: Book Club Associates, 1974, p. 15.
15. Dodd, *Elizabethan England*, p. 20.
16. Elizabeth Burton, *The Pageant of Elizabethan England*. New York: Charles Scribner's Sons, 1958, p. 27.
17. Quoted in Ivor Brown, *How Shakespeare Spent the Day*, p. 154.
18. Dodd, *Elizabethan England*, p. 85.
19. Quoted in Lacey Baldwin Smith, *The Horizon Book of the Elizabethan World*. New York: American Heritage, 1967, p. 272.
20. Dodd, *Elizabethan England*, p. 172.
21. Schelling, *Elizabethan Drama*, vol. 1, p. 100.

Chapter 2: Enter the Playhouse

22. Dodd, *Elizabethan England*, p. 158.
23. Schelling, *Elizabethan Drama*, vol. 1, p. 153.
24. Anne Terry White, *Will Shakespeare and the Globe Theater*. New York: Random House, 1955, p. 35.
25. White, *Will Shakespeare and the Globe Theater*, p. 36.
26. Martin Holmes, *Elizabethan London*. New York: Frederick A. Praeger, 1969, p. 80.
27. Quoted in Horizon, *Shakespeare's England*, p. 75.
28. Schelling, *Elizabethan Drama*, vol. 1, p. 159.
29. Quoted in Schelling, *Elizabethan Drama*, vol. 1, p. 161.
30. Hodges, *Shakespeare's Theatre*, p. 55.
31. Horizon, *Shakespeare's England*, p. 38.
32. Davis, *Life in Elizabethan Days*, p. 352.
33. Quoted in Schelling, *Elizabethan Drama*, vol. 1, p. 172.
34. Holmes, *Elizabethan London*, p. 77.
35. Schelling, *Elizabethan Drama*, vol. 1, p. 177.
36. Marchette Chute, *Shakespeare of London*. New York: E. P. Dutton, 1949, p. 33.

37. Schelling, *Elizabethan Drama*, vol. 1, pp. 148, 151.
38. Hodges, *Shakespeare's Theatre*, p. 101.
39. Holmes, *Elizabethan London*, p. 75.
40. Holmes, *Elizabethan London*, p. 75.
41. Holmes, *Elizabethan London*, p. 74.
42. Quoted in Horizon, *Shakespeare's England*, p. 61.

Chapter 3: Little Better than Vagabonds

43. Quoted in Horizon, *Shakespeare's England*, p. 21.
44. Schelling, *Elizabethan Drama*, vol. 1, p. 145.
45. Ivor Brown, *How Shakespeare Spent the Day*, p. 49.
46. Horizon, *Shakespeare's England*, p. 19.
47. Quoted in Horizon, *Shakespeare's England*, p. 68.
48. Burton, *The Pageant of Elizabethan England*, p. 201.
49. Ivor Brown, *How Shakespeare Spent the Day*, p. 119.
50. Schelling, *Elizabethan Drama*, vol. 1, p. 317.
51. Schelling, *Elizabethan Drama*, vol. 1, p. 117.
52. Schelling, *Elizabethan Drama*, vol. 1, p. 116.
53. E. K. Chambers, *The Elizabethan Stage*, vol. 1. Oxford: Clarendon Press, 1923, p. 350.
54. Schelling, *Elizabethan Drama*, vol. 1, p. 179.
55. Quoted in Hodges, *Shakespeare's Theatre*, p. 80.

Chapter 4: Groundlings and Six-Penny Gallants

56. Horizon, *Shakespeare's England*, p. 81.
57. Quoted in Ivor Brown, *How Shakespeare Spent the Day*, p. 29.
58. Burton, *The Pageant of Elizabethan England*, p. 195.
59. Burton, *The Pageant of Elizabethan England*, p. 197.
60. Quoted in Burton, *The Pageant of Elizabethan England*, p. 199.
61. Holmes, *Elizabethan London*, p. 82.
62. Quoted in Charles Norman, *Christopher Marlowe: The Muse's Darling*. New York: Bobbs-Merrill, 1971, p. 109.
63. Horizon, *Shakespeare's England*, p. 82.
64. Quoted in John Dover Wilson, ed., *Life in Shakespeare's England*. Cambridge, England: Cambridge University Press, 1956, p. 170.
65. Quoted in Alfred Harbage, *Shakespeare's Audience*. New York: Columbia University Press, 1941, pp. 77–78.
66. Quoted in Smith, *The Horizon Book of the Elizabethan World*, p. 136.
67. Quoted in Harbage, *Shakespeare's Audience*, p. 75.
68. Holmes, *Elizabethan London*, p. 96.
69. Burton, *The Pageant of Elizabethan England*, p. 124.
70. Quoted in Burton, *The Pageant of Elizabethan England*, p. 94.
71. Ivor Brown, *Shakespeare in His Time*. Edinburgh: Thomas Nelson & Sons, 1960, p. 121.
72. Burton, *The Pageant of Elizabethan England*, p. 246.
73. Quoted in Davis, *Life in Elizabethan Days*, p. 85.
74. Quoted in Ivor Brown, *How Shakespeare Spent the Day*, p. 80.
75. Horizon, *Shakespeare's England*, p. 65.
76. Horizon, *Shakespeare's England*, p. 65.

Chapter 5: Stars of the Stage

77. Smith, *The Horizon Book of the Elizabethan World*, p. 129.

78. Quoted in Chambers, *The Elizabethan Stage*, vol. 2, p. 325.

79. Quoted in Chambers, *The Elizabethan Stage*, vol. 2, p. 345.

80. Quoted in Chambers, *The Elizabethan Stage*, vol. 2. p. 344.

81. Chambers, *The Elizabethan Stage*, vol. 2, p. 342.

82. Quoted in Chambers, *The Elizabethan Stage*, vol. 2, p. 343.

83. Quoted in Martin Banham, ed., *The Cambridge Guide to World Theatre*. Cambridge, England: Cambridge University Press, 1988, p. 547.

84. John Russell Brown, ed., *The Oxford Illustrated History of Theatre*. Oxford: Oxford University Press, 1995, p. 189.

85. Quoted in Chambers, *The Elizabethan Stage*, vol. 2, p. 326.

86. Phyllis Hartnoll and Peter Found, eds., *The Concise Oxford Companion to the Theatre*. Oxford: Oxford University Press, 1992, p. 71.

87. Banham, *The Cambridge Guide to World Theatre*, p. 133.

88. Quoted in Chambers, *The Elizabethan Stage*, vol. 2, p. 308.

89. Quoted in Chambers, *The Elizabethan Stage*, vol. 2, p. 296.

90. Chambers, *The Elizabethan Stage*, vol. 2, p. 298.

91. Quoted in Chambers, *The Elizabethan Stage*, vol. 2, p. 299.

92. Quoted in Chambers, *The Elizabethan Stage*, vol. 2, p. 329.

93. Schelling, *Elizabethan Drama*, vol. 1, p. xxiv.

Chapter 6: The Many Faces of the Play

94. Schelling, *Elizabethan Drama*, vol. 2, p. 430.

95. Quoted in Smith, *The Horizon Book of the Elizabethan World*, p. 143.

96. Davis, *Life in Elizabethan Days*, p. 211.

97. Schelling, *Elizabethan Drama*, vol. 1, p. 359.

98. Schelling, *Elizabethan Drama*, vol. 1, p. 394.

99. Marchette Chute, *Ben Jonson of Westminster*. New York: E. P. Dutton, 1953, p. 175.

100. Schelling, *Elizabethan Drama*, vol. 1, p. xxxix.

101. Quoted in Holmes, *Elizabethan London*, p. 33.

102. Quoted in Schelling, *Elizabethan Drama*, vol. 1, p. 475.

103. Schelling, *Elizabethan Drama*, vol. 1, p. 553.

104. Burton, *The Pageant of Elizabethan England*, p. 200.

105. Schelling, *Elizabethan Drama*, vol. 2, p. 183.

106. Schelling, *Elizabethan Drama*, vol. 1, p. 288.

107. Schelling, *Elizabethan Drama*, vol. 1, p. xxix.

108. Chute, *Ben Jonson of Westminster*, p. 27.

109. Schelling, *Elizabethan Drama*, vol. 2, p. 93.

110. Quoted in Schelling, *Elizabethan Drama*, vol. 2, p. 105.

111. Quoted in Chute, *Ben Jonson of Westminster*, p. 140.

112. Quoted in John Russell Brown, *The Oxford Illustrated History of Theatre*, p. 200.

113. Quoted in Chute, *Ben Jonson of Westminster*, p. 325.

Chapter 7: "This Horde of Writers"

114. Schelling, *Elizabethan Drama*, vol. 2, p. 373.

115. Ivor Brown, *How Shakespeare Spent the Day*, p. 14.

116. Schelling, *Elizabethan Drama*, vol. 1, p. 316.
117. Quoted in Schelling, *Elizabethan Drama*, vol. 1, p. 336.
118. Chambers, *The Elizabethan Stage*, vol. 3, p. 324.
119. Quoted in Chambers, *The Elizabethan Stage*, vol. 3, p. 324.
120. Quoted in Horizon, *Shakespeare's England*, p. 48.
121. Schelling, *Elizabethan Drama*, vol. 1, p. 238.
122. Norman, *Christopher Marlowe*, p. 25.
123. Quoted in Norman, *Christopher Marlowe*, p. 108.
124. Norman, *Christopher Marlowe*, p. 69.
125. Quoted in Banham, *The Cambridge Guide to World Theatre*, p. 529.
126. Quoted in Schelling, *Elizabethan Drama*, vol. 1, p. 488.
127. Quoted in Schelling, *Elizabethan Drama*, vol. 2, p. 376.
128. Chute, *Ben Jonson of Westminster*, p. 67.
129. Chute, *Ben Jonson of Westminster*, p. 33.
130. Schelling, *Elizabethan Drama*, vol. 1, p. 270.
131. Ivor Brown, *How Shakespeare Spent the Day*, p. 8.
132. Horizon, *Shakespeare's England*, p. 116.
133. Quoted in Schelling, *Elizabethan Drama*, vol. 2, p. 379.
134. Quoted in Horizon, *Shakespeare's England*, p. 137.
135. Frank Ernest Hill, *To Meet Will Shakespeare*. New York: Dodd, Mead, 1949, p. 467.
136. Quoted in Chute, *Ben Jonson of Westminster*, p. 275.

Epilogue: The Elizabethan Heritage

137. Ivor Brown, *How Shakespeare Spent the Day*, p. 54.
138. Schelling, *Elizabethan Drama*, vol. 2, p. 431.

For Further Reading

A. H. Dodd, *Elizabethan England*. London: Book Club Associates, 1974. Detailed description of Elizabethan society that covers life at court, in the country, at school, and at home. Contains a chapter on arts and pastimes, with references to the theater.

Marzieh Gail, *Life in the Renaissance*. New York: Random House, 1968. Emphasizes Renaissance life in Italy, but covers details of dress, work, and play in England as well. Includes many period illustrations.

C. Walter Hodges, *Shakespeare's Theatre*. New York: Coward-McCann, 1964. Writing in conversational style, Hodges covers the development of the Elizabethan theater from the time of the miracle plays to the burning of the Globe theater in 1613.

Horizon Magazine, ed., *Shakespeare's England*. New York: American Heritage, 1964. Readable overview of the Elizabethan theater, including performances at court, players on tour, the effect of plague on the theaters, and compilation of the First Folio of Shakespeare's plays.

Sue Lyon, ed., *Shakespeare's England*. New York: Marshall Cavendish, 1989. Children's picture book that is packed with interesting information and excellent illustrations on Elizabeth I, England, and the Elizabethan theater. Includes sidebars on such topics as the Spanish Armada.

Works Consulted

Janet Arnold, *Patterns of Fashion*. London: Macmillan London, 1985. Visual overview of clothing worn by Europeans between 1560 and 1620. Contains photos and descriptions of authentic Elizabethan garments as well as patterns for reproducing them.

Martin Banham, ed., *The Cambridge Guide to World Theatre*. Cambridge, England: Cambridge University Press, 1988. An encyclopedia of the theater. Includes brief biographical summaries of important actors and playwrights, as well as descriptions of theaters, dances, theater companies, and more.

Ivor Brown, *How Shakespeare Spent the Day*. New York: Hill & Wang, 1963. A valuable source of details of life in the Elizabethan theater, including the players' daily routines, their training, how much they earned, and more.

———, *Shakespeare in His Time*. Edinburgh: Thomas Nelson & Sons, 1960. A personal look at Shakespeare, the theater, and life in London during the Elizabethan era.

John Russell Brown, ed., *The Oxford Illustrated History of Theatre*. Oxford: Oxford University Press, 1995. Complete study of the theater from its beginnings to the present day; contains a chapter on the English Renaissance theater.

Elizabeth Burton, *The Pageant of Elizabethan England*. New York: Charles Scribner's Sons, 1958. Covers details of the queen's early life and other prosaic but fascinating topics such as cosmetics, jewelry, toys, and toothaches.

E. K. Chambers, *The Elizabethan Stage*. 4 vols. Oxford: Clarendon Press, 1923. An advanced four-volume reference set that discusses all aspects of the Elizabethan theater. Includes hard-to-find details on the lives of actors and playwrights.

Marchette Chute, *Ben Jonson of Westminster*. New York: E. P. Dutton, 1953. Well-written biography of bricklayer-turned-playwright Ben Jonson.

———, *Shakespeare of London*. New York: E. P. Dutton, 1949. A readable account of Shakespeare as a working member of the London theater. Includes excellent descriptions of life in London.

William Stearns Davis, *Life in Elizabethan Days*. New York: Harper & Brothers, 1930. In conversational style, Davis discusses the manners and customs of ordinary Elizabethans, including marriage, medicine, superstitions, sports, and playgoing.

Douglas Gray, ed., *The Oxford Book of Late Medieval Verse and Prose*. Oxford: Clarendon Press, 1985. Contains information on Elizabethan grammar and spelling.

Alfred Harbage, *Shakespeare's Audience*. New York: Columbia University Press, 1941. Focuses on the social status, behavior, and expectations of the Elizabethan audience. Moderately difficult reading.

Phyllis Hartnoll and Peter Found, eds., *The Concise Oxford Companion to the Theatre*. Oxford: Oxford University Press, 1992. An encyclopedia of the theater. Includes brief biographical summaries of actors, playwrights, and theaters in Elizabethan times.

Frank Ernest Hill, *To Meet Will Shakespeare*. New York: Dodd, Mead, 1949. An analysis of Shakespeare as a playwright. Includes a section that discusses the question of Shakespearean authorship of the plays.

Martin Holmes, *Elizabethan London*. New York: Frederick A. Praeger, 1969. Features original maps of London during Elizabeth's reign. Includes chapters on professional entertainment, crime, and punishment.

————, *Shakespeare and His Players*. New York: Charles Scribner's Sons, 1972. Thorough study of various aspects of the Elizabethan play, including disguise and recognition.

B. L. Joseph, *Elizabethan Acting*. London: Oxford University Press, 1951. Contains interesting information on rhetorical conventions in Elizabethan drama. Difficult reading.

Norah Lofts, *Queens of England*. New York: Doubleday, 1977. Contains brief but informative chapters on selected English queens, including Mary Tudor and Elizabeth I.

Charles Norman, *Christopher Marlowe: The Muse's Darling*. New York: Bobbs-Merrill, 1971. The life story of playwright Christopher Marlowe. Difficult reading for readers with no prior knowledge of Elizabethan events.

Laurence Olivier, *On Acting*. New York: Simon and Schuster, 1986. Insights and experiences of a renowned modern-day Shakespearean actor.

Alison Plowden, *The Young Elizabeth*. New York: Stein and Day, 1971. Readable biography by a British author who covers Elizabeth's tumultuous early life up to her coronation.

A. L. Rowse, *Christopher Marlowe: His Life and Work*. New York: Harper & Row, 1964. A straightforward, fact-filled biography of the Elizabethan playwright.

Felix Schelling, *Elizabethan Drama 1558–1642*. 2 vols. Boston: Houghton Mifflin, 1908. Detailed and authoritative account of Elizabethan drama from Elizabeth's rise to the throne in 1558 through the closing of the theaters in 1642. Difficult reading.

Lacey Baldwin Smith, *The Horizon Book of the Elizabethan World*. New York: American Heritage, 1967. Excellent overview of Elizabethan England, including numerous maps and illustrations, short overviews, and lengthy articles. The book covers a wide range of topics, from parliamentary speeches to advice on choosing a wife. Contains a short section on the theater.

Anne Terry White, *Will Shakespeare and the Globe Theater*. New York: Random House, 1955. Written in an outdated style, this account of Shakespeare's career as a playwright is based partly on fact and partly on educated guesswork.

John Dover Wilson, ed., *Life in Shakespeare's England*. Cambridge, England: Cambridge University Press, 1956. Interesting collection of prose and poetry written during and shortly after the Elizabethan era. Includes topics such as education, superstitions, and rogues and vagabonds.

Index

Picture Credits

About the Author

Diane Yancey began writing for her own entertainment when she was thirteen, living in Grass Valley, California. A graduate of Augustana College in Illinois, she now pursues a writing career in the Pacific Northwest, where she lives with her husband, two daughters, and two cats. Her interests include collecting old books, building miniature houses, and traveling.

Ms. Yancey's books include *Desperadoes and Dynamite*, *The Reunification of Germany*, *The Hunt for Hidden Killers*, *Life in War-Torn Bosnia*, and *Camels for Uncle Sam*.